Small Dragons

Edited by Owen Godfrey, Danny Daines, Moyukh Muzahid

This book was produced as a collaborative effort between all the following authors, each of whom are a stakeholder in the final work, and therefore share the copyright of the overall publication. The editors act to coordinate the interests of these authors regarding this publication. Each author retains the original copyright of their story, which is reproduced here with their permission as a part of the overall work.

The artwork # has been provided by <u>Stephen Landry</u> (http://sxcore87blog.wordpress.com).

The artwork * has been provided by <u>DC & JL Daines</u>

The Secret Santa Initiative,
https://www.facebook.com/SmallDragons
mailto:Secret.Santa@nomdejoy.com

Table of Contents

Foreword

BY **D.C. DAINES**

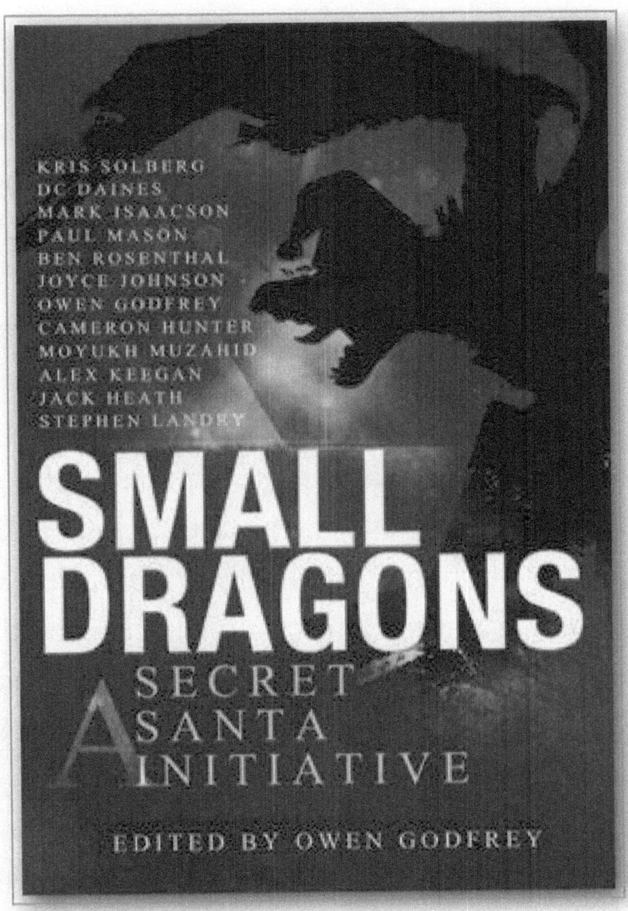

Secret Santa Initiative.

I met Kris at Swancon, a local convention in Perth. He brought my book from me and then proceeded to stalk me online, trying to get me to read his stuff. No seriously. He introduced himself and asked if I could have a read of his short stories as he had read my blog where I had suggested that someone who was not emotionally invested in your work should have a read and give an honest opinion. I said yeah, no probs. Weeks later, when I had lost the stories in the multitude of other work I had going on, he asked me again. Yay for me, as I was honest and explained I had lost them with my marbles. He sent them again. I immediately read them before I had time to lose them again and was pleasantly surprised as they were well written and really entertaining.

After many of his little stories, he pitched me the idea of the anthology. Get someone else to pitch an idea of what they would like in a short story, character, plot, conflict and get you to write it. Times that by a few published authors of the different arts and a few unknowns that would like to get some experience in the field of writing and I thought it would be a success. However I do not write short stories. Blah. Poetry is as close as I get. Well, an opportunity like this does not come up every day so armed with the dread of having to come up with a short story we began searching for participants and we found a great selection of people and talents I am proud to be in this compilation with. Now funny enough, writing the short story was the easy part for me. Coming up with an idea that was interesting, not done a million times before, malleable to one's own style and above all else entertaining, and on top of it all, an idea that you were happy to give away for someone else to write? NOT EASY. After that hurdle came the writing, and if that was not enough, we were smarty pants and wanted a linear connection to the anthology, apart from the main theme and without restricting our styles too much. Well, this is where Owen Godfrey came in. Taking an idea and pitching it where it would do the most damage. At me. The Small Dragon. That was it. Every story must include the phrase, The Small Dragon. Nothing more, nothing less. I jumped for glee. Anyone that has read my stuff would know why. Funny enough after all the fuss we put up about The Small Dragon, many of us, including myself, completely forgot the concept until later.

The concepts seem to have worked out very well for the little group we have formed, the stories both entertaining and different and I am hoping that in the future we have more projects to contribute towards. One I have been throwing around with other authors from the anthology would be to write our own ideas, the ones we were so quick to throw at our poor peers this time around. I have also found it interesting that so much creativity can come from the same idea. Thus, I believe it would be fun pitching two authors against each other and give them the one idea to write.

Future projects aside, this was fun, the people awesome and Kris a worthy originator. Owen Godfrey took the lead, followed by Mohamed and guidance by Stephen Grin made the editing of this anthology less of a chore and more of a learning experience I intend to take away with me.

Thank you so much for this opportunity to entertain you.

Jasmine

BY BEN ROSENTHAL

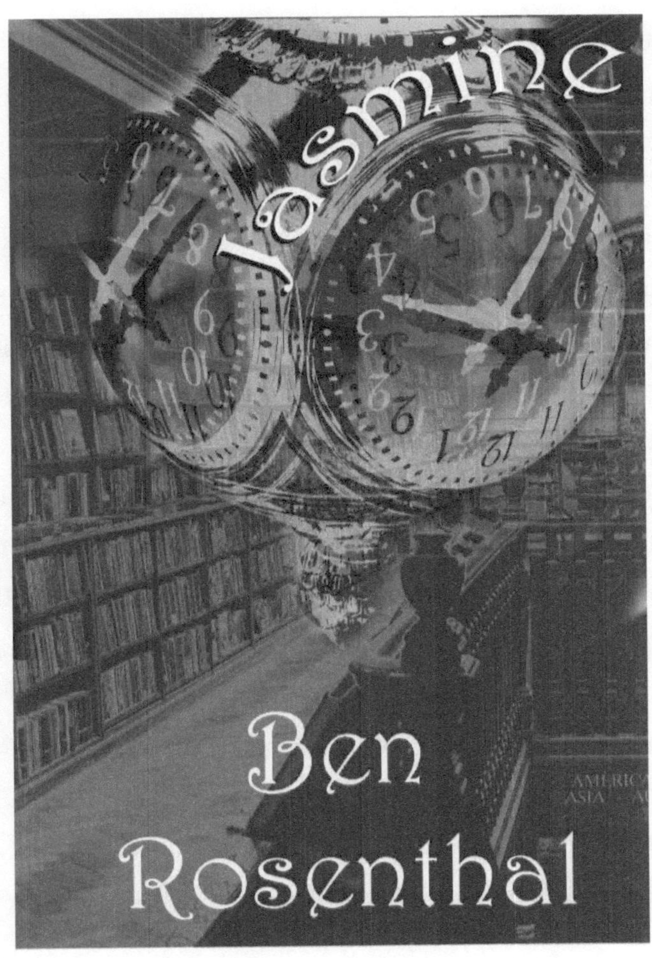

I wish that I'd never met her.

If I had never met her I know I wouldn't be here now. I know I would not be standing in the thundering rain, looking at these vicious waves below wondering why I actually came and what to do next.

I wouldn't have been led here by this photo; her photo.

How long do I wait?

I do know why I went into the library that day. In the city with an hour to kill, looking at books seemed a good way to slay it.

As I entered the grand old building, the waft of decaying paper brought a smile to my face. I stood in the old doorway looking at the vast rows of shelves housing the knowledge of the ages. The chairs in the middle of the large hall were empty. The silence of the library was broken only by the dull roar of a heater, which no longer held up its end of the bargain. A rather large, suited man sat at the welcome desk, looking up purely to acknowledge my existence then returning his gaze to the book in hand. Smiling, I walked into the main room. I passed the chairs and wandered into the stacks — hundreds of tomes resting upon the rows and rows of bookshelves greeted me. Looking at this maze I was reminded of the first time I had come to the library. As a first year university student, I had become lost and couldn't find the exit. Not actually lost. More disorientated; nobody gets lost in a library.

I began to walk the aisles, not looking for anything in particular but waiting for something to catch my eye.

Faded words on cracked leather spines begged at me to grab them. To open them and read the tales they had to share. Looking on in hope as I walked towards them. Disappointed as I passed them by. Of course I speak metaphorically; books do not have eyes. However a gap between two of them did.

It wasn't an illustration or a figment of my imagination. A human eye looked back at me from the next row over. Someone was spying on me (or possibly checking me out). I bent down and looked at it. Long lashes blinked as I stared into the ice blue color of their iris. "Hello?" I said (Not the most original thing to say, I know, but being in a library I felt the need to stick with the classics).

"Hi," replied a confident female voice. I was taken aback. Why was there a female watching (checking me out) me from the aisle over? "Are you spying on me?" I asked. Better to get that question out of the way first. With any hope it would elicit a laugh from my mysterious stalker. My ego flexed as a lovely chuckle came from the other side.

"Only a little bit. But it's for a very good reason I assure you."

"And what reason is that?" I grinned. This female was very quickly intriguing me more than the dying volumes of text we were surrounded by.

"Meet me out front and I'll tell you," she replied. And with that the eye was gone. I heard footsteps quickly walk away. "How will I know who you are?" I called after her, to no reply.

I simply shrugged and made my way towards the exit. This time I did not have any problem finding it.

I began looking for her the moment I stepped out the doors. However in my rush I forgot a very simple fact — there are more than just two people living in this city. Men and women, children and their pets walked up and down the footpath going about their lives. Half a dozen females alone stood near the library entrance.

A few were looking around anxiously for friends, while others played with their phones in an attempt to look like they weren't feeling incredibly self-conscious and exposed being by themselves. I had no idea what to do. I had no idea who the woman in the library was. I did not know what she looked like, how tall she was or what she was wearing. All I had to go on was a single brilliant blue eye.

I've never been one to take chances. I play it safe — collect data and make an informed decision based on research and discoveries. Today would be no different. I would take my time to survey the situation. To think about how much time had elapsed between her leaving the building and me exiting. I would take into account the weather conditions. As it was a sunny but cold day the probability of her choosing to stand in the open was high. That gave me better statistics to work... and then I thought 'bugger it'.

I walked up to a girl who was standing around, looking as if she were waiting for someone. Yes, I do admit that she was probably the prettiest one that I could see at the time, but I was not thinking that specifically. I was in unfamiliar territory. I had no facts to back me up. I was naked (not actually naked).

"Hello…?" I asked, cautiously.

"Um, hi," replied the girl. I tried to look her in the eye to see if it was the one which had looked back at me before. I must have stared too intently as she quickly became uneasy and asked me to leave her alone in a way that was not befitting of her beauty. Luckily her eyes were brown.

As the good-looking girl walked away a voice came from behind me; one that I knew would be accompanied by an eye of the iciest blue I had ever seen. "Very smooth,

Mr. Preston," she said as I turned to face her. She was not what I expected.

Shorter than me, this girl wore a dress which looked like it came from the 1950s with leather boots from today. Her hair was bright pink and stood up in a faux Mohawk. Her face was like that of a porcelain doll — pale and fragile — which made her bright blue eyes stand out all the more.

"How did you know my last name?" I asked. "Who are you?"

"That's not important," she replied as she looked at her watch, anxiously.

She handed me a picture. "Do you know where this is?" she asked me hurriedly. I took the picture from her hands and studied it. It was a photo of the ocean taken from a cliff face. "I don't know. I think... maybe".

"Three weeks. In three weeks be where this picture is. I have to go." And with that I once again heard the hurrying footsteps. Looking up from the picture I could see she was already a few lengths ahead of me. However this time I was going to follow her. "Wait," I cried. "I don't even know your name".

"Jasmine" she yelled back. I continued the chase. I needed answers now, not in three weeks time.

Who was she? How did she know my last name and why did she give me this picture? So focused on the pursuit

I did not notice the frame of a rather large suited man from the library. I crashed into him. Hard.

I fell to the ground — he did not even seem to notice the impact. "Are you ok?" he asked as I picked myself up off the ground.

"Yeah," I replied as I looked around for Jasmine. I had lost her.

"Perfect."

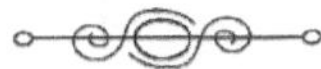

It took me a few weeks to find the exact location of her picture. It was in a book near where we first spoke. Seems it wasn't such a random encounter after all. So here I stand, a crumpled photo in my hand and listening to the waves crash against the rather pointy rocks far below me. That's probably why I didn't hear the footsteps coming up from behind me.

"David Preston," a voice boomed from behind. I turned quickly to see a man in a suit. The man from the library; the man into whom I had bumped when chasing Jasmine.

"What's going on here?"

"We are glad you made it," the suited man says as he takes a step closer towards me.

"Now hang on just a minute," I start, suddenly feeling very threatened being in between this large individual and the pointy rocks far below. "I have no idea why you are here or what is going on. I just came because I was told to. A girl called Jasmine wants me here."

"I know," he says as he takes yet another step closer to me. "She sent me here to greet you."

"Huh?"

"Don't worry Mr Preston," the suited man calmly says as he places his hands on my shoulders. "Just let your body go limp." And with that the suited man shoves me off the cliff.

…

It's a weird feeling knowing that you are about to die. People talk about seeing their whole life flash before their eyes. How the major moments are played out in your mind for you to relive. The girl you first loved. The puppy who meant the world to you. All I could think about was how unfair this was and that I think I have peed my pants.

There was nothing left that I can do. I am falling to my death. I close my eyes and wait for the rocks to break my body apart.

THUD. Ouch.

A sharp pain in my right elbow confuses me. Shouldn't there be more pain? Shouldn't I be in a million pieces right now? Then I feel a floor under me; smooth and not in the least bit jagged or rocky. I think I am still alive, I think to myself. Either that or the afterlife smells like a garage — a garage where tacos were the primary food source. Opening my eyes slowly confirms that I have not fallen to my doom, but rather into some kind of metal room. Computer monitors line the walls. Flashing lights highlight symbols that I have not seen outside of an episode of Doctor Who.

"Sorry about the dramatics," a female says from my right. Even though I have no idea where I am, I know exactly whom the voice belongs to.

Jasmine steps into my line of vision, offering me her hand. I glare back at her for a short time, finally deciding that I can get up without her help, thank you very much. I have no idea what is going on or why, moments ago, I had been pushed to my death only to turn up here — wherever 'here' is. All I know was that she is responsible for it somehow.

"What. The. Hell."

"I know you're upset, but I only did what needed to be done to ensure you were ready," Jasmine tells me calmly. She does not seem surprised at my reaction.

"Ready? Ready for being pushed off a cliff? Ready to buy a new pair of pants? Ready for being... wherever the hell here is. Ready for what?"

"Ready," continues Jasmine, "to save all of reality."

She walks over to a control desk under the large screen. Pressing a few buttons, the picture fades to show the vast sea that I was staring at not ten minutes ago. "Are we — are we in a spaceship?" I ask foolishly, not actually believing those words were leaving my mouth.

"Strap yourself in David," said Jasmine as she continues to tap at buttons, not looking away from the large screen for an instant. "You've got a lot work to do."

Awestruck I settled myself in a chair next to her. Two words on the dash of the 'ship' caught my eye.

"What's 'Small Dragon'?" I ask.

Jasmine smiled as she threw a lever. "That's what you are about to find out."

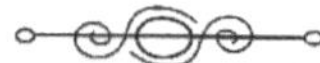

Concept idea given to authors to write story = A man stands on the edge of a cliff contemplating his life as he readies himself to jump

Ben Rosenthal was born from a young age. His hobbies include reading, writing and referring to himself in the third person.

You can see more of his words at ManInSuitComics.com, benjum.com or hassle him over on twitter: @BenRosenthal.

Beneath the Surface

BY KRIS SOLBERG

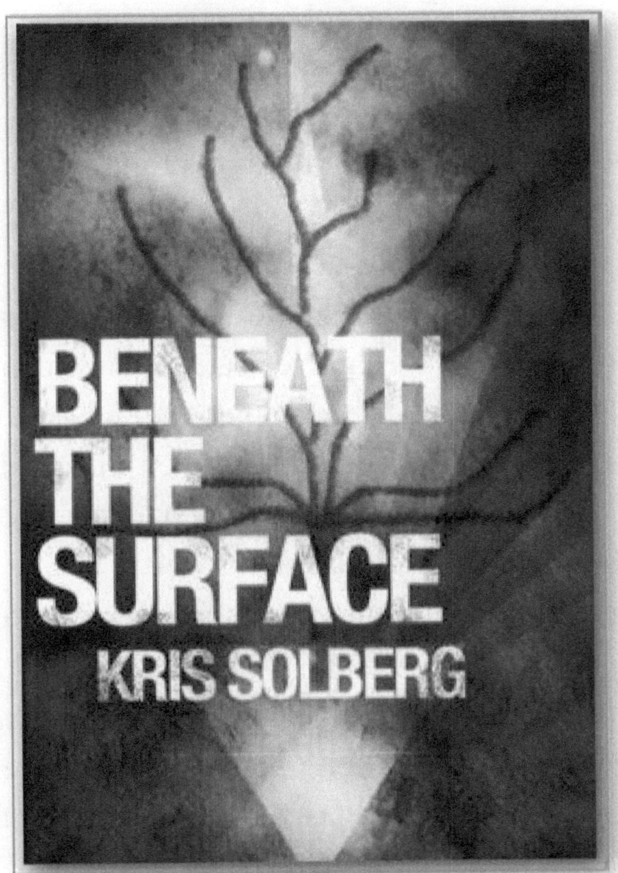

In a small village, not too far from where you're sitting right now, there's a circular formation of houses, about twenty or so. Quietly they all rest, neatly tucked away for the night as the cold winter air roars through the blackness around them. All are asleep, apart from one little house standing at the far right of the circle, slightly askew from all the rest. The dark blue boards blend morosely with the terrorizing evening air, the aphonic color stands apart from the brightly painted houses surrounding them.

The entire village is asleep apart from three people, three people waiting for the darkness to go away, waiting patiently, yet it never does. The youngest of the three is a little girl by the name of Clara Billingsly. Clara is six years old, she has long flowing blonde hair, an endearing face and a desire to explore every creek and cranny of the world she resides in. The other two people in the house are her parents, Fiona and Clark Billingsly. They are keeping little Clara awake, stopping her from exploring the world beyond her own in her dreams, as they are yelling at each other, crying out into the silent, indifferent breeze of winter.

Clara is used to them yelling, as they have done so ever since she was born. With her very first step she tried to walk away from her parents, yet they are always there to drag her back to the life within the four dark walls of the house they live in. Clara has never fully understood what her parents argue about. There's a lot of screaming, paper flying through the air, paper with massive red letters stamped all over them.

She has tried to spell them out, and in her effort she declares majestically, manifesting herself in every letter; "O-V-E-R-D-U-E", she reads another, passionately declaring every word with the strongest sense of urgency her little self can muster, "E-V-I-C-T-I-O-N". She knows the letters but not the words. Whenever she tries to ask her parents, they dismiss her with a snarly tone, condemning her curiosity to the far-reaching depths of her mind.

While she has grown accustomed to falling asleep to the sound of her parents arguing, drowning out the noise, like a sailor rocking himself peacefully to sleep on the mighty foam waves of a wide and uncharted ocean, there is something missing; something that has been a soothing comfort from the terrors outside her whitely painted wooden door with a poster of a beautiful princess in a pink dress.

She sits up in the bed, rubbing her drowsy eyes gently as she looks around the room. "Are you there?" she whispers peacefully, almost dreaming the words as they drop off her tongue. The darkness has no reprieve from the silence, only the muffled groan of her parents fighting beyond the hallway, deep within the belly of the house.

With a determined reach, she stretches across her bed, towards her night stand, flicking on a small lamp, lighting up the lamp-shade with Woody and Buzz from Toy Story looking up at her, helping her search the room for her lost friend. "You can come out now," she mutters gently as she checks under her bed before she waddles over to her closest.

She places all her strength into her arms and pushes the sturdy door of the closet open, allowing the light from the Toy Story lamp to consume the darkness waiting for her inside. A thick row of dresses, shirts, skirts, and more look back at her, yet she turns away with a frustrated sigh, the kind of sigh that sells a thousand words in a single gush of air.

As she returns to the bed, nuzzling herself tightly under her Princess Bubblegum bed sheets, she turns off the Toy Story lamp with a reluctant gasp as she says "Why don't you like me any more?"

The darkness consumes the room, yet its reign is short lasted. Within a few passing moments a thin, light blue haze starts dancing around the room, flickering gently between the strands in her blinds. As she notices the color, she jumps up from her bed, jolting over to the window. With a determined crack, she peeks through the blinds and looks down at a dimly lit horizon at the clearing behind her house, behind a thick tree line, down by the narrow creek running alongside the village.

"I knew he wouldn't leave me" she screams to herself as she squeezes her feet into her pink boots, a pair that's at least two sizes too small yet she doesn't have the courage to ask her parents for a new pair.

She nuzzles the frazzled ends of her cotton pyjamas into the shoes and climbs out of the window. It's only a one story house so her room is close to the ground, it's a climb she's done hundreds of times, sometimes with help but she's learned how to do it on her own lately. First she steps onto the chair standing next to the window, a placement her parents are yet to question, then she opens the window wide, before she climbs onto the window sill and jumps into the awaiting embrace of the freshly fallen snow below.

The flakes leap into the sky as she drops into the dune of snow under her window. It's a warm, affectionate embrace and she sits there for a moment, enjoying the caressing warmth of the snow around her, before she gets up and starts running towards the creek.

As she enters the tree line she hears the sounds she has been waiting to hear all day. It's a quiet clatter, a muffled stampede of feet running through the snow.

The blue light dominates the scene as she escapes the choking deafness of the trees. Her eyes dance between the small creature sitting, waiting for her by the creek and the blue spaceship standing along the shoreline, its calming blue lights welcoming her back.

"Scratches, you're back!" Clara declares joyfully as she runs towards the little creature sitting by the water. It remains quiet by the creek as she runs up next to it, crouching down before she embeds herself around its neck. "What took you so long?" she asks demandingly as she lets go.

Her eyes stare into the bleak expression of her friend, sitting by shore with seemingly nothing to say. She looks down at the figure, clearly lit up by the blue lights of the spaceship. It looks like a mixture between a dog and a bear. Its four, sturdy legs blend seamlessly with the thick, fluffy fur covering its body. The head dips in solemn thought as Clara stands up in front of it.

From the altered angle she sees a stream of rainbow colored liquid running from its bottom left paw towards the water, merging amorously with the white snow before draining into the creek, a thinned out, softly colored liquid.

"Scratches", she says with a puzzled grin, "what's happened? What is that?" She looks down at the liquid, trying to work out what has happened to her friend. "Scratches, say something." With a gentle nudge she pushes the furry creature into the snow. The cold sting of the powdered whiteness wakes it from its haze. It shakes imperiously before looking at Clara.

"I can never come back" The words are spoken with silent reluctance. The furry creature buries his gaze deep within the crystal blue eyes staring down at it. "Clara, I can never come back."

The little girl looks confused down at the creature as it drags itself out of the snow. It shakes ferociously for a moment, banishing the snow into the cold winter air once more. The creature starts walking towards the spaceship, leaving little rainbow footprints as it walks away. Clara remains silent for a moment, before jolting after it. "Scratches, wh-why can you never come back?"

The furry creature stops by the blue spaceship. It looks sternly into the snow, its fluffy growth wincing in the cool winter breeze. "Because of you, Clara. I can never come back because of you."

A walking pad sinks down from the ship. Above, Clara can only see a bright light engulfing whatever hides inside the spacecraft. Scratches takes a step onto the pad before turning, looking warmly back at the little girl. Clara stands silently with a confused gaze. A single tear is streaming down her rosy cheek. "Please, Scratches. Don't leave me." The single tear is joined by a flood of emotion as Clara takes a step towards the walking pad. "N-not you too."

Rainbow colored liquid is slowly seeping from the walking pad, blending timorously with the white snow.

Scratches looks down at the blood leaving his body before staring up at Clara. "I have to, Clara. I can't stay here. I'm risking everything just by coming to tell you this." Scratches shifts its gaze to Clara, it's a confrontational stare as it bores its sight into the pleading eyes of the little girl.

"Look at me, Clara. You are doing this to me. Your belief in me is dwindling, dissipating, slowly disappearing. I know it's not your fault. You can't help it, it just happens." The furry creature turns away from the weeping girl as it takes another step up the walking pad. "But I need to find someone else to believe in me, someone new that can restore me."

Clara falls down pleading in front of Scratches, feeling the cold from the snow drill past her cotton pajamas. Her eyes are breaking from the strain of tears forcing themselves out. She stammers silently, before reaching for her furry friend. "P-ple-please. Don't leave me. I promise, I'll believe in you again. I'll never doubt you. I p-pr-pr-romise!"

Scratches turns reluctantly, his eyes sell compassion and understanding for what the little girl is going through, yet his expression is stern. "No, Clara. Your doubt is spreading even as you speak. Your emotions betray you, the real you. You don't believe any longer, Clara. As you sit there in front of this ship, feeling the cold embed itself in your body, your confidence in me and everyone around you is disappearing. I have tried to stand by you for as long as I could but my presence here is only weakening your own resolve."

Scratches pushes Clara off of the platform and watches as she falls acquiescently into the snow. She stares up at her friend as the light from the ship engulfs the furry tassels of its being, its final shade gleaming out of the brightness like a small dragon.

"Be strong, Clara. The world will not be strong for you." are the last words that escape from the ship before the port slides shut.

Clara rests calmly in the snow, watching as the ship disappears into the night sky. She lets the cold consume her body as well as her mind. The cotton pajamas battles bravely against the freezing winds but eventually it cannot sustain its struggle.

The sun peaks up from the mountainous surroundings of the village, welcoming the start of another day. The village slowly awakes from its slumber, the residents clearing their driveways of last night's snowfall. Chasing the snow away with shovels and brushes, the village slowly emerges from beneath the white blanket covering the peaceful community.

What hides beneath the untouched darkness of nature? The remains of a life cut short, of dreams squandered and wasted. A girl abandoned by everyone, even herself. Resting under a blanket of icy indifference, her screams are deafening, her tears are earth shattering, her sobs are breaking. The world moves without her.

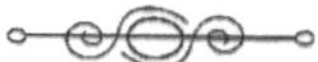

Concept idea given to authors to write story = Every night since Clara was a very small child her four-legged imaginary friend Scratches would appear by her bedside and watch over her as her parents screamed and argued. Clara is now eight years old. Her parents are arguing again and this time Scratches hasn't appeared by her side to watch over her. She sneaks out her window and wanders into the woods. She finds Scratches limping near what appears to be a massive alien spacecraft. When she begins to explore with the help of a hurt Scratches she discovers she is not alone. Something or someone has been following her.

Kris Soldberg is an Author with a passion for exploring the dark corners of his mind through writing.

Evidence

BY J ACK H EA TH

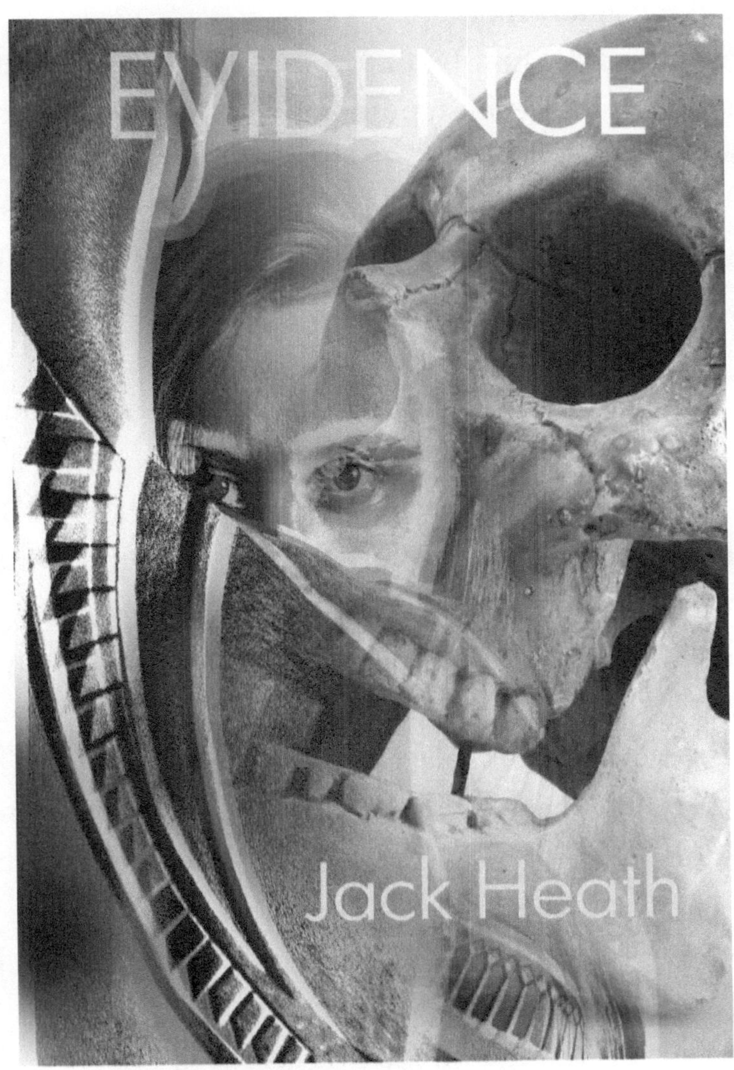

"No," Bianca hissed. "No, no, no!"

She tilted her husband's head back, pinched his nose, and pushed another lungful of air into his mouth, but his flesh already felt lifeless against her fingers.

She wouldn't give up; she knew the ambulance would be there at any moment.

She gave him two more breaths and then returned her hands to his chest, pumping so hard she heard his ribs creak.

"Come on, Derek." She tried to stop her voice from trembling, as though she could bring him back to life with confidence alone. "Wake up."

Derek didn't react. How long had he been sprawled on the polished wooden floor before she found him? What if he was beyond help?

She thumped his chest with renewed vigor. The man who flirted with her at university, who knelt on the dirty ground with an engagement ring because the top of the Eiffel tower was closed, the man who wept with joy when he saw their son squirming on the ultrasound – this man wasn't going to die today.

A mechanical dragon, one of Derek's projects, waddled toward its maker. The aluminum joints gleamed in its swishing tail. Bianca batted the small dragon aside, pressed her lips to Derek's and exhaled once. Twice. Three times.

Sirens howled on the breeze.

"They're coming, baby," she whispered, tears stinging her eyes. "Just a little longer, okay? Just breathe."

Derek's flesh was going as grey as his hair.

"Mum?"

Bianca turned to see Simon standing in the doorway, his eyes wide under his unruly black curls, his schoolbag on the floor beside him.

"He's not breathing," she said. "Help me!"

Simon stood frozen on the threshold.

Bianca was about to shout at him when the doorbell rang. "Never mind," she said. "Get the door! Go!"

Simon disappeared. Bianca kept thumping Derek's chest.

"Don't die," she begged. "Please don't die."

The paramedic bustled in, her scrubs dark from the rain outside. She was a middle-aged woman with hard eyes and a pointed chin. Crouching over Derek, she pressed a finger do his neck.

"How long has he been like this?" she asked.

"At least ten minutes," Bianca said. "That's when I found him."

Behind her, an android pushed a gurney through the door. It moved quickly and efficiently, wasting not a single joule of energy. Its face — two cameras, a speaker, two microphones and a USB port — was inscrutable.

"Hippocrates, load him up," the paramedic said.

The android slid two multi-jointed arms beneath Derek and lifted him with a barely audible whirring sound. Derek's limbs flopped lifelessly as he was placed upon the gurney. His jaw hung open.

Bianca ran her hands through her tangled blonde locks, breathing heavily as the android pushed the gurney out of the room. Simon followed, staring at his father's slack features.

"Is he allergic to anything?" the paramedic asked.

"What?"

"Any allergies?"

"Oh. pseudo-ephedrine," Bianca said. "I think that's it."

"Okay." The paramedic held out a tablet and a stylus. "Sign here."

Bianca scribbled a shaky signature.

"Will he be okay?" she asked.

"We'll know more at the hospital," the paramedic said. Then, after hesitating: "But you should prepare yourself for the worst."

The paramedic left the room. Bianca felt like she'd swallowed a bowling ball.

Hospital, she thought. Got to go to the hospital.

She rummaged through Derek's things, looking for his car keys. Pushing aside gears, batteries and motherboards, she finally found them next to the 3D printer. She turned to leave—

And found the doorway blocked by two tall, broad-shouldered men. Their suits were a little loose, as though they'd both lost weight since buying them.

"Mrs Park?" one of them said.

"We'd like you to come with us," the other continued.

Bianca shook her head vigorously. "I have to go to the hospital," she said. "My husband—"

One of the men flashed a badge. It read Detective Farris. "It's important."

"Well, I – let me just tell my son."

"He left in the ambulance with your husband," Farris said. "We'll drive you to the hospital to see him. Later."

As she followed them out, Bianca saw Farris marveling at the height of the ceiling and the artwork on the walls.

"You have a lovely home," he said.

Bianca wasn't sure why, but his voice left chills slithering down her spine.

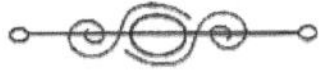

The interrogation room had the odor of bleach and old paper. Bianca couldn't smell the mug of tea, which had been placed in front of her. It was too weak. The chattering from the rest of the police station had been silenced as soon as the thick steel door swung closed.

The other detective – the one who wasn't Farris – was named Higgins. His cheeks were coated in greying stubble, and his ear had a hole where an earring had once perched.

"And you can't think of anyone who would want to hurt your husband?" he asked.

"I already told you, no," Bianca said. "Can I see him yet?"

Higgins avoided the question. "His robots are brilliant. I have one of his chef droids in my apartment. You don't think one of his competitors might have–"

"Might have done what? Broken into our house and pushed him over?"

"Does that seem likely to you?" Farris asked, apparently seriously.

"No. Everybody liked him. Everyone. He even got on well with his competitors. They admired him."

"Your husband had quite a temper," Higgins said. "Didn't he once punch a judge at an award ceremony?"

"He was—" Bianca's brain caught up with her mouth. "Wait. He had quite a temper?"

Farris glared at Higgins.

"He's dead?" Bianca cried. "Are you telling me Derek is dead?"

Farris cleared his throat. "I'm sorry," he said. "But the paramedics couldn't resuscitate him on the way to the hospital."

Bianca stared down at her murky reflection in the tea.

"We came as soon as you phoned the ambulance," Higgins said, "because a year ago, police were called to a domestic disturbance at your residence."

"I wasn't home," she said, quietly.

"So Derek said. Apparently he was on a conference call. The neighbors heard him shouting."

"That's right." Derek is dead, Bianca thought. Derek is dead.

"Or maybe you were home," Farris put in. "And you hid, so the police wouldn't see your bruises."

"Bruises?"

"Maybe he assaulted you. Perhaps not for the first time. And last night you decided enough was enough."

"What are you talking about?"

Farris rose to his feet and put his palms flat on the table. "You put pseudo-ephedrine in his food. You knew he was allergic. You waited until he had stopped breathing before you called the ambulance–"

"No," Bianca said. "I loved Derek. I would never–"

"Then who did? If everyone liked him, as you say?"

Someone knocked on the door and opened it without waiting for an invitation. It was a woman with cherry-red hair, wound into a tight bun. She looked Bianca up and down twice.

"We're with a suspect," Farris growled.

"No you're not," the woman said. "According to the polygraph, there are only two heartbeats in here." She pointed at Bianca. "That's an android."

Bianca looked over her shoulder, as though someone else was in the corner. But no – the woman had pointed at her.

'I'm sorry?' Farris said.

The woman shrugged. "So am I. But that's not a suspect. Not even a witness. That's evidence."

"That's ridiculous," Bianca said. "I'm not – hey!"

Higgins grabbed her wrist. She tried to pull away, but his grip was too tight.

"No pulse," he said. He peered curiously into Bianca's eyes. "It looks so lifelike."

"Of course I'm lifelike!" Bianca protested. "I'm alive!"

The cops ignored her. "How did this happen?" Farris demanded.

"The wife of a brilliant roboticist turns out to be a robot?" the woman said. "Gee, I wonder."

"But she has a driver's license. A home loan. A taxpayer number. You need a birth certificate to get those things."

"I have one," Bianca said. Her heartbeat was deafening in her ears. For the first time, she wondered if the sensation was artificial.

No, she told herself. I'm a human being.

"I'm guessing the real Bianca Park died some time ago," the woman said. "This is a duplicate."

"You think her husband recreated her out of grief?" Higgins asked.

"Or one of his competitors killed her," Farris murmured. "And replaced her with a replica to spy on him."

"I want to see my son," Bianca said.

"Now we've got two deaths to investigate instead of one," Higgins said. "Where do we even start?"

"I don't want to tell you how to do your jobs," the woman said, "but perhaps you should start with the evidence."

"I want to see my son!" Bianca screamed.

The cops all looked at her.

"He's not your son," the woman said. "I've already called child services about placing him in foster care." She turned immediately back to the two detectives. "It takes a long time to download information out of a human brain, even one with an implant. But getting data out of an android's hard drive should be fairly straightforward."

"I'm pretty sure it's told us everything it knows," Farris said.

"Then pull its body apart. The serial numbers on the components will help you find out who built it, and when. That may not tell you who killed Bianca and Derek Park, but it'd be a good start."

She walked out, and let the door fall closed.

Bianca raised her trembling hands.

"Okay," she said. "Let's talk about this."

The two detectives lunged at her.

Higgins went for her left arm, Farris for her right. She managed to dodge Farris, but not Higgins. She cried out as Higgins's meaty hand crushed her flesh.

"Stop!" she begged.

Higgins didn't stop. He dragged her toward the door. Farris opened it, and then followed as Higgins hauled her out.

The police station wasn't as loud as before. Most people had gone home. A dispatch operator spoke into a headset. A cop had a muscular youth handcuffed in a chair. A woman in a neat suit — possibly a lawyer — lounged nearby.

You have the right to an attorney, Bianca thought. But I don't.

Higgins pulled her toward the cellblock — and her arm popped off.

Bianca was shocked, but not as much as Higgins. He stumbled backward, off-balance, clutching her severed arm like an Olympic torch. The titanium socket shone under the neon lights.

Farris tried to grab Bianca's other arm. Too slow. She whirled around and hit him. His nose crumpled under her metal knuckles.

Higgins dropped the arm and dived after her, but she was already out of reach, sprinting toward the exit.

The other cop abandoned the handcuffed youth and moved to block her way. He lifted a can of capsicum spray and depressed the release valve.

A blast of orange mist hit Bianca in the face. Suddenly she couldn't see, but there was no pain.

She kicked at where she thought the cop's crotch was, and heard him collapse, wheezing. Wiping her eyes, she stepped over him and dashed out the front door into the night air. Thunder boomed above. Rainwater dotted her cheeks. She ran.

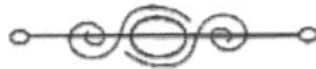

It was risky, coming to the hospital. Other than her house, there was nowhere else she had any reason to go. If the cops had half a brain between them, this was the first place they would check.

But Simon was her only living relative. Even if she wasn't biologically his mother, she still had memories of giving birth to him, bouncing him when he cried, holding his hand as he took his first shaky steps. And he was all she had left of Derek.

Once Simon disappeared into the foster system, she'd never find him. Not with the police looking for her.

She crept along the polished tiles, peering into each room as she passed it. Her hand trailed along the safety rail that lined the corridor. Her missing arm was concealed under a jacket she'd found draped over a chair in the foyer.

What if Simon was gone already? The cops said Derek was dead before he reached the hospital. How long would it take for the Department of Child Services to send someone to pick Simon up?

All she could do was hope.

A nurse walked past, smiling. She glanced at the empty sleeve, but didn't pause. Bianca guessed that missing limbs were a common sight here. She smiled back. The nurse moved on.

A maze of colored lines marked the floor, leading the way to different departments; yellow for radiology, red for pathology, green for pediatrics, and so on. Simon was a teenager, almost an adult, but only pediatrics sounded remotely right, so she followed the green line.

The walls of the pediatrics wing were painted with cartoon characters – thinly veiled rip-offs of existing properties, like Mikey Mouse, Bob the talking sponge, and similar. Bianca walked past the receptionist, trying to look as though she knew where she was going. The receptionist didn't look up from her magazine.

She saw his face through the glass. Simon was sitting alone on one of many brightly colored chairs. Discarded toys for toddlers littered the carpet around him. He stared at the wall, as impassive as the android that had carried his father away.

Bianca pushed open the door. Simon looked up at her.

"I had to do it, Mum," he said. "He killed you."

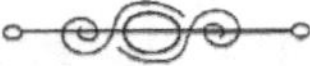

Jack Heath is an Australian writer of young adult fiction, best known for his book Money Run. He has been shortlisted for the Nottinghamshire Brilliant Book Award, the Aurealis Sci-Fi book of the Year, the National Year of Reading "Our Story" Collection and the Young Australian of the Year Award. He lives in Canberra.

A Debt Repaid

BY JOYCE P JOHNSON

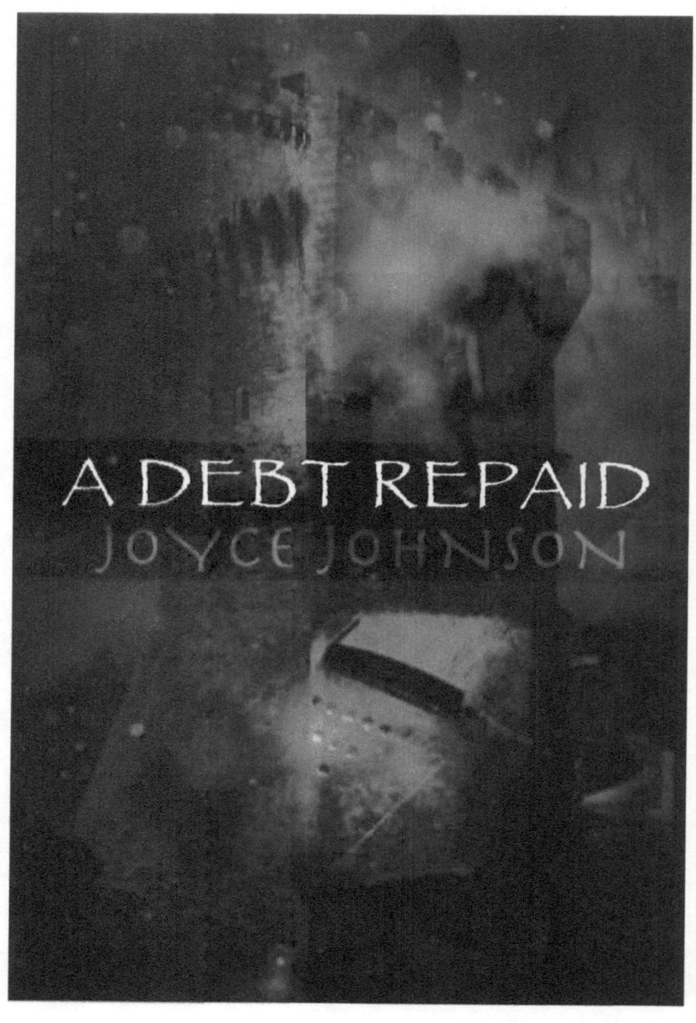

The fire smoked in the crisp evening air, he turned from the dwindling coals, his eyes as black as the night sky. He tried to make out his surroundings; this was not the place he remembered, something had gone wrong.

He attempted to cast his mind back to happier times to when this place meant something to him; to when his parents and sister were still part of his life. A small smile creased his mouth and cheeks as the memories flooded back... He could see them all enjoying this place, enjoying each other's company without a care in the world, thinking this was how it was to be forever. How wrong they were... how wrong he had been. How arrogant to believe the troubles that surrounded them would pass them by; that they were untouchable somehow. However the scene that now confronted him reminded him of his arrogance, his egotistical outlook and how his family depended on him. Their survival was his responsibility; just as their death would be of his making.

His name was Kaeden and he was the first-born and therefore heir to his father's kingdom. The kingdom stretched further than the eye could see, it contained wooded forests and rocky mountains. A river flowed through its heart and branched off into streams along the way. Streams that watered the crops and help feed his people. At the center of this realm stood the King's castle, like a beacon to all, as a symbol of protection and benevolence. The king was an understanding and generous monarch who had carried his people through war, harsh winters and fire and they not only loved him but respected him. Kaeden wanted more than anything to be just like his father, to follow in his footsteps. This journey should have begun with his coming of age challenge but instead here he sat surrounded by devastation. It was his duty to defend the realm, his people and his family and if that meant sacrificing himself then that would be the price paid. He could never have imagined this scenario when his father had encountered the old man on this very road...

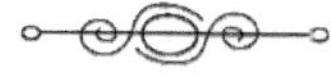

THREE MONTHS EARLIER

It was a magnificent summer day. The rays of the sun warmed all they touched and lit up the world with a brightness that promised everlasting life. As they basked in its light they knew they were the chosen, they were born to lead, they were born to protect. Frolicking on the edge of the woods and by the banks of the stream all was right in their world. They instinctively knew this was how it was meant to be and how it would stay. The King and his family rarely had moments such as these where they could enjoy each other's company, relax and feel the benefits of their station. The previous years had been hard with many battles fought and many harsh winters endured but they had survived, his kingdom had survived and now began to prosper again. His daughter, Wysteria, was soon to be wed and his son Kaeden was about to undertake the biggest challenge of his life, he had to prove his worthiness to inherit the throne. King Ferrar and his wife, Lady Eoron, were confident of his success he had been trained well and had performed well in battle leading the charge in many skirmishes. However, for now he just wanted to enjoy this time with his family and forget the past as well as the coming challenges. He wanted to be in the moment and savor this precious day and all it promised.

The guards stood on sentry as the family huddled onto the blanket that had been carefully laid on the ground, and helped themselves to the sumptuous picnic that surrounded them. These were the spoils of their kingdom. Each morsel had been grown or bred on their lands and prepared by their cook; this would be their last gathering for some time and they all wanted to enjoy these simple pleasures, pleasures they had been brought up with. Their father had encouraged his children to make the most of the simple things in life, not to flaunt their position and to appreciate the people over whom they ruled, because as he muttered many times; *without a people to reign over you cannot be a king. You are simply a person of noble birth, treat them well and respect them and they will respect you.* The people not only respected and loved King Ferrar but they loved all of his family as well. They would gather to witness Kaeden undergo his challenges and cheer him to success just as they had done for his father.

As the day drew to a close the family prepared to make their way back to the castle content in mind, body and soul. It had been a good day and they were refreshed. The guards commenced the procession but no sooner had they started, they came to a standstill. The King descended his coach to enquire of the problem and without a word being uttered he was immediately aware of a problem. All the guards, the horses, the carriages were frozen almost in mid-step. He heard a noise and abruptly turned around to see his son alighting the coach.

"Stop Kaeden," he called. "Something is wrong, stay with your mother and sister while I investigate."

"No, Father," he replied with his hand on his sword. "I must come with you, to protect you."

"No," was his reply as he too unsheathed his sword and held it out in front of himself. "Your mother and sister must be protected. I can fend for myself."

With that Kaeden stood by the coach, guarding his family as his father ventured to the front of the procession in an attempt to ascertain the problem. Slowly he crept, ever aware of his surroundings glancing from side to side; he took each step cautiously, deliberately. The trees themselves also appeared to be frozen. There was not a sound to be heard, the world was in limbo with the King and his family the only things able to move. Unsure of the origin of this phenomenon the King's mind was flooded with theories all impossible and unbelievable, but the truth of the matter was staring him in the face and he was preparing himself to come to terms with it, whatever IT may be.

As he reached the front of the procession there appeared to be an old man lying on the ground, the King immediately put his sword away and ran to his aid.

"Are you alright, what can I do for you?" he hastily enquired.

The old man smiled and slowly rose, looked the King in the eye and announced "No, it is I who can help you."

"Help me? I do not understand."

"Yes help you. Look around. It appears a spell has been cast over your kingdom, far and wide this scene is being repeated. All your subjects, your animals, your lands are frozen in time. Do you know how to unfreeze them?" he asked with a sly grin across his face.

"A spell, how do you know it is a spell and that it extends across my kingdom? Did you cast this spell, did you cause this problem?"

"Me?" he replied swiftly, "I am just an old man, how could I create such a problem? I am feeble and weak, incapable of such trickery."

"Then how is it that you know how to undo this spell if you did not cast it?"

"A very good question," said the old man, "I wonder if Kaeden knows the answer... or maybe he knows the solution to your problem... or perhaps he is the solution. Where is your son? Bring him to me!" he commanded.

Shortly after Kaeden made his way to his father and was confronted by the old man "Kaeden, you have grown up well, strong and handsome, come closer so I may inspect my goods."

Kaeden was puzzled, what was this old man going on about "What do you mean '*your goods*'? I am the son of the King; I belong to my people, not one old man."

"Yes I am sure that is what your father told you, but maybe he forgot the deal he made many years ago when his bride could not conceive a child," he said as he turned to the King. "Did you forget Your Highness, that moment of despair when you whispered a declaration to the universe?"

"I do not know of what you speak," the King warily replied.

"Come now do not be shy..." the old man said as he materialized a mist in the sky containing the scene. "Surely you remember vowing to pay whatever price necessary to have an heir?"

There amongst the mist was a figure kneeling on the ground with his face forsakenly resting in his hands. Sobs of grief could be heard emanating from the figure. Then as he moved his head to face the heavens, the features of a man became visible. It was the King; a younger version but definitely the King. As he peered into the heavens he began to speak.

"Surely this is not how it is meant to be... my wife can suffer no more... she carries our child for weeks only then loses our heir... time and time again. There can be no reason for this... there must be something that can be done. I will do anything, promise anything to end this suffering... please hear my pleas and I will comply with any conditions."

Another voice was then heard, a disembodied voice softly drifts to his ears. "You will comply with any conditions? There may be a way. Would you be willing to give up your first born if I promise more than one heir?"

"Give up my first born? I do not understand exactly when would we be expected to hand this child to you?"

"Sometime in the future I will come to you and demand payment and you must comply... For this I will give you the miracle you seek... do you agree?"

"Anything... anything to end my wife's suffering. What must I do?"

"Nothing... just live your life and wait for my visit."

The mist disappeared and the King stood speechless. The look on his face showed his recognition of the scene and his body language showed the resignation to the situation.

"No! I will not be bought and sold like chattel," declared Kaeden. "I am a man and should have the right to fight for my freedom."

"Spirit and courage... I like that. You will certainly be a great addition to my family," stated the old man.

"Please be merciful," pleaded the King. "He is our son not yours, he belongs with us... do not take him from us!"

"No," boomed a voice incongruous with the frail figure that stood before them. "He was on loan to you till I was ready for him... now I am ready for him."

"I will not go... you cannot force me," Kaeden defiantly said.

"No. I will not force you. However if you refuse to comply I will leave the spell on this realm and your people will remain frozen in perpetuity."

"How can you be so cruel, do you not realize what affect this will have?" Kaeden replied.

"I was not the one who did not consider consequences," replied the old man coldly. "It was your father; he made a deal and I am now here to collect... a simple business arrangement."

"Is there no way we can renegotiate this deal?" the King asked.

"Renegotiate... that is an intriguing notion... what do you propose?"

"What do you want?" Kaeden replied quickly.

"Why I want you Kaeden... however I suppose I could maybe... just maybe... have a loan of you instead of full possession. How does that sound?"

"A loan?" queried the King "I do not understand. What sort of loan and what would the duration be?"

"Come now, let us not get into details. Suffice to say I need a favor, and if Kaeden performs this I will release you from your obligation. Kaeden, what do you say? Are you prepared to help an old man with a tiny problem and in the process release your people and satisfy your father's commitment?"

"How tiny is this problem?" queried Kaeden

"I have many enemies and one in particular has become particularly worrisome, however I believe you could help me solve the problem with little or no fuss."

"You have the power of magic, what could I do that you cannot?"

"A mortal, especially one as noble as you has many qualities I do not possess. Let us just say you fit the criteria of my dilemma better than I ever could. Do we have a deal... you do this favor for me and I release the spell? I allow your family to live and for you to stay with them. Fight me and you will be my slave, the realm stays frozen and your family dies. Sounds like an easy choice to me; what do you think Kaeden?"

"How do I know you will keep your word if I accept your deal?" Kaeden asked.

"I am an honorable man and I keep my word... unlike your father who tries to shirk his responsibility to me. As a show of faith, once you have accepted, I will release the spell BUT your family will stay with me to ensure you successfully complete the quest. Do we have a deal on the word of two gentlemen?"

"You leave me little choice; however I need to know what happens to my family if I am unsuccessful."

"They die of course. I cannot have you not trying your hardest to win can I now?"

"I accept your terms, but I do need to know what this quest you require of me is."

"All in good time my boy. Firstly I need you to bring your sister and mother to me. Once I have them, I will unfreeze the realm, and you will come with me."

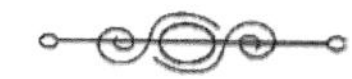

PRESENT DAY

At that time little did Kaeden realize what the old man expected of him and how it would ravage the countryside of his realm. As he surveyed the desolation that surrounded him, he knew this was to be his final stand, the next few hours would determine not only his fate, but also that of the family he held so dear and the kingdom he always assumed would be his one day.

He was tired... so tired every muscle in his body ached and the many wounds that had been inflicted seemed to burn into his very flesh. The countryside was blackened and all his people were hiding, too scared to show their faces or offer any attempts of resistance or help for him. He was alone. In his mind he kept images of his family... reasons for this battle; solace in this dark place that once was his home. In the past month he had called upon these images to give him inspiration, to give him the will to continue and now as his body fought fatigue and pain, he needed inspiration more than ever. He needed a minuscule glimmer of hope that he could be victorious. Victory was such a hollow word in these circumstances; victory should be cause for celebration but all he wanted was to rest, to lie down and forget any of this had ever happened; to allow his body and soul to repair and be made new again.

He felt himself drifting off to sleep but all the time knowing that sleep would never come; sleep was a refuge, an escape and his enemy would not allow him such a luxury. As the images of his surroundings became dimmer and the noises were suppressed in his head, he felt a presence beside him. His warrior instincts heightened, and he jumped to his feet, immediately alert, surveying all around him to determine what had caused the disturbance in his psyche.

Initially he saw nothing but he still 'felt' a presence. Becoming even more alert he continued his surveillance and then behind a charred tree he saw it. At first it was only an impression that soon became an outline and the longer he stared, features became clearer.

"Who goes there?" he clearly shouted.

"It is only me," someone said in a small, low-pitched voice that seemed to materialize in the air. "I have come to help you."

"Show yourself... come forward and show yourself!" Kaeden commanded.

"I am afraid you may hurt me," the voice declared with a slight hint of fear. "Please believe me I am only here to help."

"I will not harm you," Kaeden continued, "but show yourself now."

As he peered into the darkness he saw the shape make its way from the remains of the large tree. The first recognizable feature Kaeden could make out were two large round eyes that appeared to glow in the darkness, then as the form made its way toward him he was taken aback... should he be scared or take the creature at its word and believe it was there to help?

A small dragon slowly walked toward him and the scales that covered its body seemed to be luminescent in the darkness of the night. It was slightly taller than Kaeden but its length was almost double its height.

"Who or what are you," Kaeden skeptically queried, "and why have you come... in fact where have you come from?"

"My name is Kilo and I am here to help," the dragon slowly and cautiously replied. "The monster that you fight killed my mother and I need help to defeat it... I thought we could help each other."

"If this monster killed your mother and I assume she was bigger, stronger and more battle ready than you, how do you expect to defeat it?"

"I do not... but I believe WE can," he confidently stated. "We both have special skills that when combined will not only surprise but defeat our nemesis."

"Really? In that case I think we need to talk. Tell me what you can bring to the battle."

"I can fly... I can fly you... I can help you surprise this beast," Kilo confidently stated. "I can maneuver you into a winning position. With my ability and your fighting skills, we will be victorious and avenge my mothers' death."

"How did you hear of my dilemma and where have you come from?" Kaeden queried.

"I lived with my mother in the caves beyond the mountains; it is part of your kingdom so in effect I am one of your subjects," Kilo said with a giggle. "Your quest is well known within your realm and my mother attempted to assist you by attacking the beast, but alas after many battles it proved too strong and she succumbed to her wounds. I observed her battle strategy and also that of the beast, so I can instruct you before and during the battles and I know we can be victorious," Kilo proudly pronounced.

"You are so young and so small, how could you improvise a winning strategy?"

"I am older than I look and my mother taught me well. My size will work to your advantage as it also makes me agile, much more so than your opponent. I can sweep behind it and you can attack him unawares... trust me... we can win and your family will be freed."

"I really do not have a choice so I welcome you into my battle. Let us work out our plan and tomorrow we will start a new era... an era of freedom and salvation."

The next morning both Kaeden and Kilo rose early, ate a hearty breakfast and started to implement the plans they had laid out the previous night. They had decided to surprise the beast with Kilo. Kaeden would approach the battlefield alone as he had done so many times before and call the beast out. He would strike the first foray at the beast and as he retaliated, Kilo would swoop down and scoop up Kaeden, taking him far into the sky above the beast and out of sight. Then at the appropriate time they would both plunge down and attack the beast when he least expected it.

As Kaeden approached the field he felt an extra spring in his step, his spirit was more buoyant, he was confident the plan would work... he and Kilo would be the victors and the beast would lay slain on the ground and his family and realm would be free forever.

Kaeden yelled to the beast to show himself to confront his enemy, and face his destiny. Out of the shadows the beast appeared, somehow it seemed smaller today, or maybe Kaeden was more confident. Its scales glistened in the sunlight while the eyes, as black as night, stared him down. The strong jagged tail flicked in the air as the beast readied itself for the fight. As it spoke a collar of spines displayed themselves around his neck and his long tongue, usually throwing fire, dripped with saliva.

"You speak confidently for a man who is to face his death," the beast announced. "I grow tired of this charade, tired of your inadequacy. I will finish this today and you will face your destiny, your death."

"I too grow tired of these battles and I agree it must end today," Kaeden replied. "Give me your best and we will see who faces their death."

With that a mighty paw came sweeping down aimed at Kaeden, but with his renewed energy he was able to dodge it and instead of being injured he landed a blow with his sword to the upper quadrant of the beast's paw. Keaden felt the flesh tear under his blade. Blood started to spurt, and Kaeden jumped to one side and in completion of his motion the sword caught the other side of the paw. Again his blade sliced through sinews and muscles and he knew these blows would cripple the beast.

Kaeden jumped back inspecting the damage he had inflicted and waited for the beast's next blow. However before it could connect, Kilo flew down and scooped Kaeden up, the move was so sudden and so unexpected the beast fell back in shock and stared as they disappeared into the sky. The beast shot a plume of smoke and fire after them, but they were too quick.

Adrenalin pumped through Kaeden and Kilo. They felt invincible. Their planned move had been successful and Kaeden's blows to the beast had inflicted severe wounds. As they soared into the abyss they were already formulating their next move. This time they had to be more careful, the beast was aware of Kilo's existence now so he would be prepared.

As they circled, they could observe the beast's movement below, however the beast was oblivious to theirs as it did not know where to look and they used the available cloud cover as camouflage. Slowly and silently they came around ready for their next move, waiting till just the right moment to strike. Confused, the beast clumsily moved around, hindered by his severely injured foot, searching the heavens for his prey. They were nowhere to be seen. Then, just as the beast moved into position, they dove down. Kilo aerodynamically positioned himself to move fast without wind resistance, Kaeden lying flat matching Kilo's stance, but with his sword positioned ready to insert into the backbone of the beast. His intention was to fracture the beast's backbone and make him immobile. S-W-O-O-O-S-H they went, and the wind they created was their only signature. Kaeden embedded the sword up to its hilt into the flesh that ran along the beast's backbone. Blood and sinews spluttered from the wound. Then, without releasing his hold on the sword, Kaeden steadied himself as Kilo swiftly flew in a straight line dragging the sword along with him. Kaeden again felt the flesh give way to his blade but this time he also felt the crunch of bone as the beast's backbone succumbed. Then without a moment's hesitation, Kilo changed direction as Kaeden released the sword and they soared upwards. As they rocketed into the sky Kaeden glanced backward and saw the beast fall. The trees around it shuddered as it fell and it landed flat on the ground surrounded by its own blood.

Kilo hovered for a moment as they both surveyed the scene below, watching, waiting, for the beast to stir. There was nothing, not even a muscle in that enormous body flickered. The stillness of the beast's end was eerie, not a sound was uttered, not a bone cracked or a sinew twisted. It just lay there still and silent unable to cause any more harm, unable to kill anyone else's mother. Kilo silently smiled to himself and then turned to Kaeden.

"We have done it," Kilo proudly announced. "We have done as I promised... together we have brought an end to the reign of terror this beast has inflicted on your kingdom."

"Yes," Kaeden jubilantly replied, "my friend we have. Against all odds together we have triumphed, and you will always hold a place of honour in my court."

Kilo slowly made his way to the ground so they could inspect their kill, and ensure the beast was truly dead. As they walked around the dead carcass, it seemed smaller than Kaeden had remembered when fighting it. Yes smaller indeed. In death this animal was inconsequential, just a means to an end. Kaeden silently wondered why he had been in such awe of it, why had he been so intimidated by it. It was merely flesh and blood, and as it lay lifeless on the ground, it was good for nothing except food for other animals.

Kaeden mounted the carcass, and made his way to the top, where he retrieved his sword from the flesh of this inanimate menace. Holding the sword aloft he yelled to the skies.

"Old man I have done your bidding... the beast is dead... you are now free of him. Come and fulfill your end of our bargain. Return my family and be gone from our shores."

Staring into the blue sky he saw a mist appear, and then the apparition of the old man.

"You have done well Kaeden," his voice boomed from the heavens. "However not entirely on your own I see. Who is your little friend?"

"This is Kilo and his mother was killed fighting the beast," Kaeden cautiously declared. "He joined with me to avenge her death. You made no mention of this quest having to be completed by me alone."

"You are right my boy, and as I said I am a man of my word. You have done as I have asked and you will be rewarded. You are free, your father's debt to me is clear. Your family will be returned to you and you will never hear from me again... unless of course you summon me."

"Summon you!" Kaeden declared. "Why would I ever summon you? My father made a deal with you at a moment of weakness and vulnerability and it could have destroyed my life and my family. His failing has taught me to be wary of people who take advantage of current circumstances, I will never be so naive," he boldly stated.

"Do not be so quick to discount the possibility; you do not know what the future holds. The future is a wondrous thing with many twists and turns and one day... yes, one day, you may be in need of my assistance," the voice softly stated. "When... or if... that day comes do not hesitate, as I feel I am now in your debt."

"That day will never dawn," Kaeden declared with such certainty. "I would rather die than to become beholding to you. I prefer to place my faith and future in the hands of one who declares their interests and has as much to gain from a venture as I do," he said as he placed an arm around his new friend. "I believe that is the basis of a true alliance and perhaps friendship, not deceit and tricks."

"You are young. When you are older, more experienced, you will learn nothing is that absolute. However I wish you well my young friend and my offer remains if your circumstances or outlook may change I will hear you."

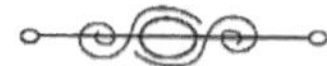

Concept idea given to authors to write story = The fire smoked in the crisp evening air, he turned from the dwindling coals, his eyes as black as the night sky. He tried to make out his surroundings, this was not the place he remembered, something had gone wrong.

Joyce P. Johnson is 59 years old and married for 38 years with two grown very successful children.

Her first published novel was 'Genesis of Memory', book one of the Genesis Saga. She is currently working on 'Genesis of Betrayal', which was preceded by 'Genesis of Life', 'Genesis of Destiny', and 'Genesis of Love', all of which will shortly be available. You can follow the progress of the Genesis Saga on its Facebook page 'Genesis of Memory'.

Joyce P. Johnson bas been writing since she was eight years old. Writing for her was an escape, a refuge, a place she could imagine all types of wondrous things.

The Incident at Owl Pass

BY JAMES HUNTER
AND
OWEN D. GODFREY

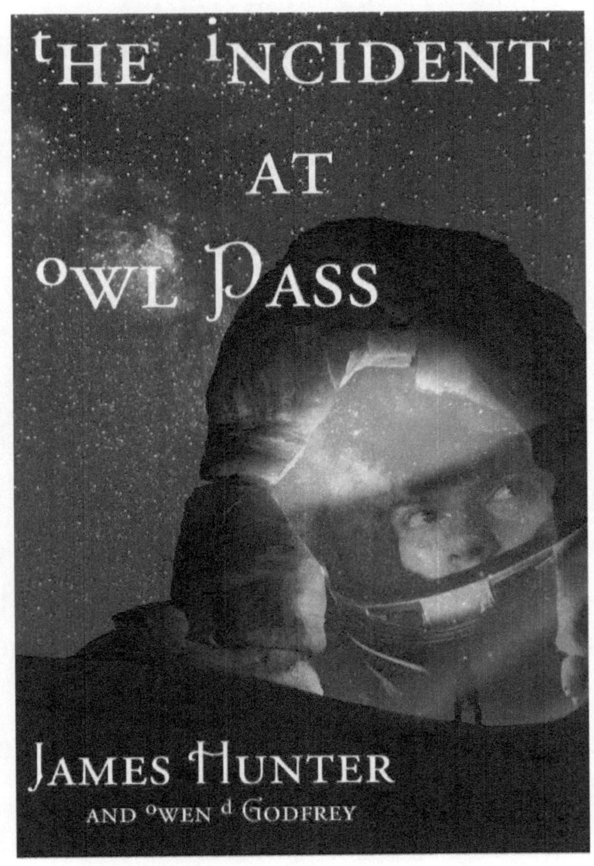

The Smallest Dragon raced along the wide track, just entering Owl Pass. Desert dust pin-wheeling around the blue glow of her engines. Within its cramped cockpit, Aaron Tate was hunched at the controls, his face lit by the drive-system readouts. Surrounded by dangling wires and bare metal, he listened to the vibrations of the engines through his fingers. Minute shudders made him frown, but he pushed her faster and faster. The racer was designed for speed, not comfort, though Aaron barely noticed the numbness in his legs or stiffness in his neck. His eyes flicked to the temperature gauge that was taped to the roof, then back to the readouts on the console. He grimaced, gritted his teeth and opened the throttle a fraction more.

Aaron glanced at the forward display, checking he was still roughly on course. In the distance towered pillars of rock, ostensibly natural, though he had no idea whether this planet had been found or made; it was not unknown for entire planets to be built for racing.

The temperature gauge started beeping as it flashed red. He glanced up and tried to adjust the power drift, and completely missed seeing the approaching rocky outcrop. The Smallest Dragon scrapped the top, and pulled violently to the left. Aaron was thrown against the wall of the cabin as the craft began a flat spin. He tried to compensate and maintain altitude, but one glance at the approaching ground told him it was too late.

The Smallest Dragon hit the ground spinning and sliding. Aaron prayed aloud as he fought for control amid blaring alarms. He watched as pieces were thrown into the air. Finally, something caught and the small craft flipped into the air, and Aaron was thrown face first in to the console as the emergency beacon activated. He had one glimpse of the port engine spinning away as he blacked out.

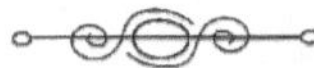

Silence...

Aaron was confused. He couldn't see anything, there was red stuff in his eyes. He realized that the power had gone when the engine was ripped off, and the only sound was the infinitely distant beeping of the emergency beacon. He was hurting all over, especially his face and hands, where blood was pooling from the g-forces of the spin...

... the Smallest Dragon hit again, and slid to a halt in a deep sand bank.

Aaron shook his head. He glanced at the temperature gauge, but it was long gone. His hand found the emergency cut-off switches and he checked that the emergency beacon was still active. It beeped at him. The cabin was a mess and he was hurting all over, and there was a red stuff all over the console and his face. He realized the console was as ruined as his face, and the red stuff was his own blood. He scrambled out of the cockpit, and ran, but the Dragon didn't explode.

Aaron's face and hands still hurt, but he was amazed he'd come out of that alive. He thought about stopping to check the wreck, but he kept running; he had to get them to come and get the Smallest Dragon and fix her up for the race in a few hours. He had no idea where the strength was coming from. In a few moments though, a hazy figure started to emerge from the darkness. As he got closer, he saw it was Sam, with the carrier bed behind her, come to collect him from the desert.

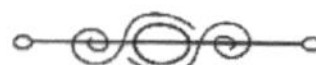

When Aaron awoke, it was to silence. He face and hands hurt, but he wasn't in his ship. Even without opening his eyes he knew this, because it was much too soft, too comfortable, and he could hear a distant beep. He could hear strange murmured noises, and a faint beeping sound, a few miles away... no, next to his head. A hazy figure swam into focus, Sam! Sam had found him.

"My ship?" he croaked. Two words, but a clear question.

"*Our* ship," corrected the young woman by the bed. "And she's fine, no serious damage."

The next second Sam was grabbing him in a hug, her short shaved hair prickly against his cheek. "Idiot," she said. "Idiot. What were you thinking?"

Aaron was aching all over and his head was thumping but he tried to explain himself. "The Dragon's been running hot lately, and I can't figure out why. It doesn't make any sense. My head hurts, could..."

"What doesn't make any bloody sense," interjected a gravelly male voice, "is why you were out at 3am flying the Dragon the morning before the last race! And for god's sake, why weren't you wearing a helmet?!" Aaron turned to see the inevitable lanky figure of his race manager, flanked by two aides.

"I'm sorry David" managed Aaron with a sinking feeling in his chest, wondering whether it was too late to fake passing back out. Unfortunately he was almost fully lucid now, and could clearly make out the stern expression on David's face.

Something went beep, and Aaron glanced around, but there was no medical equipment in the room.

"As you should be. You're flaming lucky Sam managed to guess where you might be, and who knows what might have happened if she hadn't found you." David pulled up a chair without asking and seated himself down, somewhat theatrically. His assistants remained standing by the doorway, awkwardly.

"What about the beacon? I checked that it had activated after I landed."

"Landed? You call that a landing? Anyway... the beacon's on the list now."

Aaron closed his eyes and sighed. The maintenance list was never empty. "Anyway, what do you mean she's fine? I remember pieces flying off. The port engine has to be a write-off at least."

David snorted. "You're a damn fool, but you know how to crash right. She's got some bad damage all right, and the port engine ripped right off, but for some reason the engine itself is in one piece. The frame is torn; we can either repair or replace everything with parts on hand before the race. Except the console, seems like someone tried to push their face through that. A spare is on its way."

Aaron sigh in relief.

David growled. "I'm beginning to question some of the decisions I've made, lad. Seriously question them. Our sponsors haven't heard about this yet, but could you imagine if I'd had to tell them the youngest racer ever to compete in the Series went and got himself sprayed across Owl Pass right before the final race?"

"Leave him alone, he just woke up!" exclaimed Sam from beside him. Aaron was quite surprised that she was coming to his defense, she had seemed plenty upset with him moments earlier. Though he'd often noticed there was no love lost between his mechanic and his race manager, and suddenly this was clearer than ever. David turned to Sam, an unreadable expression on his face.

"Well yeah... hell, is the Smallest Dragon going to even have a pilot in time? We can fix her up, but..."

"He'll be fine," chimed in a nurse from the corner of the room, whose presence Aaron hadn't noticed until now. She was dressed in official series "Slight bruising, laceration to the scalp, but nothing serious... the doctor thinks the blackout might have been caused by stress or shock, there's no real head injur—"

"Well. Good." David waved at her irritably. "Can you give us a moment?"

After the nurse had walked out David rounded on Aaron.

"You owe me," he said. "I got you where you are today." His expression softened slightly. "You have done well so far, really well..." he trailed off, while Sam glared at him.

"... but for the sake of... I don't know what, stop trying to get yourself killed! This race is dangerous enough and... I need the Smallest Dragon to be in the race, no matter what," said David, beckoning his aides to follow him out.

"We'll win this!" croaked Aaron as enthusiastically as he could manage, but David had already left.

Something went beep again. Aaron tried to wipe the blood from his face, but his arms wouldn't move, and everything was still spinning.

He shook his head to clear it, and then Sam drove him back to their home on the station. Although he didn't really think of their temporary quarters as home; he couldn't imagine anywhere as home, really. Over the past eighteen months, they'd stayed in as many hotel rooms and temporary quarters, each competing to be more barren and lifeless than the last. Their current accommodation was put up by the Series authority for the twelve finalists, among who were Aaron and the team of the Smallest Dragon. A small picture of a boat by some sort of fishing village adorned one of the walls. It had been two years since Aaron had been on a planet with a natural ocean.

Aaron took a deep breath. He couldn't seem to get his heart to slow down, and it was hard to breathe, and he heard that damn beep again. "Hey, forget about the room, let's go see the Dragon."

Sam nodded and drove past their rooms over to the garage. Aaron dizzily stumbled in. The Smallest Dragon stood shinily in the center of the room. She looked undamaged by his accident, undaunted. He walked over to her and somehow it became an hour later as he lay underneath the open engine and began to pull and prod at various parts.

"What are you doing," Sam asked.

Aaron jerked up and whirled around. She was still there, and must have been just standing there the whole time, eyes black with tiredness, looking at him with an odd mix of concern and anger.

"Sam..." he said slowly, "the overheating problem; It doesn't make any sense. I think output regulator's been messed with. I think somebody's trying to take us out of the race. Like... permanently" He was going over each of the other competitors in his mind, trying to think of who would be brazen enough to sabotage a racer in the Series final.

"Maybe that's not such a bad idea," said Sam, staring straight at him.

"What?

"If you could give... Aaron, you've fallen to pieces over the last year. If you could give it up now, leave it all... would you?"

"We've come so far!" he protested, confused. "And the prize money—"

"—isn't that much, after we've paid off our debts," Sam finished for him. "This is killing you Aaron, can't you see it? Hell, if you'd written off the Small Dragon, we'd be finished, in debt and no hope of digging our way out. And you'd be dead."

Aaron didn't reply.

Sam shook her head. "I have an idea," said Sam.

They made the modifications amazingly fast. Aaron had no idea how they could do all that in such a short time, but they did, even with that infernal beeping in the background. They rigged the engines to come away, burning out and catapulting the rest of the Smallest Dragon ahead. They rigged chutes to slow it and prevent a flat spin, and most of all, Sam presented him with a new helmet to protect his head.

Somehow the race began. Aaron couldn't recall how it began, but here he was in the cockpit of the Smallest dragon. It all seemed too surreal. She rounded the final curve and flew down the straight, trailing behind the leader by mere meters. Aaron hunched at the controls, coaxing as much power from the ship as he could.

When the engines finally started to groan, and the temperature and pressure readings began to spike wildly, Aaron was prepared in ways that were more than humanly possible.

Sam's voice crackled in over the radio. "Ready?" she asked, and he could hear the nervousness in her voice.

"This is crazy," he said with a grimace. Over the sound of the engine he couldn't hear the crowds outside, or the commentators, or even the sound of the other ships.

"Yeah. Shut up. Got your 'chute?"

He smiled, and opened the throttle all the way and pulled the safeties out. He shot past the race leader and across the line.

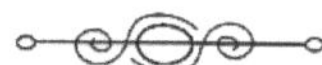

Silence...

Aaron was confused. He couldn't see anything, there was red stuff in his eyes. The only sound was the infinitely distant beeping of the emergency beacon. He was hurting all over, especially his face and hands, where blood was pooling from the g-forces of the spin...

He reached for the chute release to stop the spin, the one he had installed with Sam just an hour ago... but it wasn't there. He wasn't wearing a helmet, and he had no chute... and he was alone in the night.

An instant later the Smallest Dragon slammed into a rocky spire. The power-plant exploded in a brilliant flash that lit the morning dark, and Aaron Tate died in a lonely place called Owl Pass.

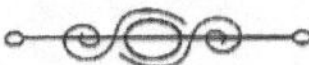

James Hunter is a 21 year old law student from Western Australia, who is an avid reader, a tea lover and an enthusiastic writer.

Owen Godfrey lives in Perth, Western Australia and has been writing stories for since he was in first grade. Even class word exercises were an opportunity to make a story to bewilder the reader. Owen has mostly written for small online publications, principally Antipodean SF, and for a number of locally published fanzines. In 2010 Owen's story "Becalmed" won third prize in the Ellen Street Recovery Group Program writing competition, and was subsequently published as a part of their anthology.

An Act of Humanity

BY JOYCE P JOHNSON

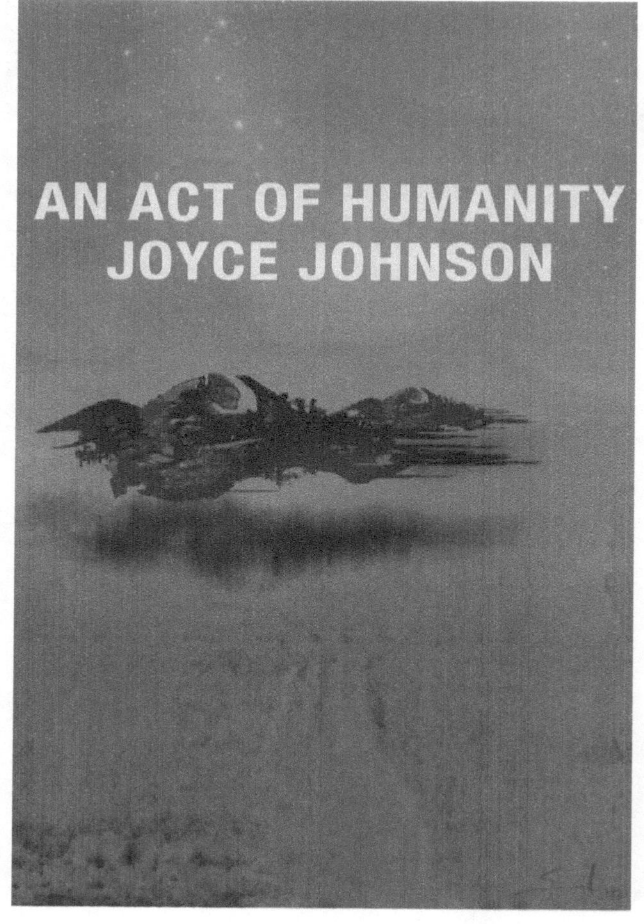

"So what do you think is going on out there?" asked Charleton as he hovered slightly above the landscape.

"Your guess is as good as mine," replied his partner Meagen, "hell we do not even know what they are researching, let alone why they have a research facility hidden underground smack in the middle of the desert."

"Yes but it must be important if they have sent three top scientists out there and they have to report in every day," stated Charleton. "Sounds like a slight bit of over kill to me."

"Maybe but if HQ want a report then a report we will give them," she answered and then they silently continued their journey.

Charleton and Meagen have been partners for two years now, not long in the scheme of things but long enough to know their lives were dependent on each other. The year is 3010 and this world is very different to the one they left behind. Their world was clean, beautiful, abundant with trees, animals and all the water you could drink, much like this world, the one they call Earth, was before the Great War and its fallout.

As they made their way to the research facility through this desolate landscape Meagen could not help but wonder what this planet used to be like. How similar to her home world before the pollution and wanton depletion of resources, before the war and the aftermath. The inhabitants had been slowly killing this world... the

War was just the final act. Now these same inhabitants paid the ultimate price, they were a lost race, hiding amongst the rubble, most disfigured by the chemicals that polluted the air immediately after, the rest too demoralized to know or care what is happening around them.

Charleton and Meagen were among the first of their race to arrive on Earth once the atmosphere cleared and the true extent of the devastation became known. They were aboard an explorer craft that came to investigate the seismic activity created by the explosions that ended life as Earth people knew it. Upon scanning the planet they discovered rich deposits of a rare element called neonate, obviously unknown to the people of Earth or they would have depleted that also. This element is a vital ingredient in an energy source used on their home planet of Cordia however it was becoming quite scarce there. Stumbling upon this find on Earth was a blessing and the fact that the people put up no resistance made the find even more valuable.

Meagen had tried to make friends with the locals but they were too skittish, afraid of their own shadow, in the end she decided to regard them much as her people did, just a curiosity, a part of the local wildlife; in fact, the only wildlife. She left food out for them on occasions but on the whole never gave them a second thought.

As they cruised along on their hover cycles they were both lost in their thoughts only occasionally giving voice to their thoughts, which mostly centered on what they would find once they reached their destination. Predators were non-existent and the locals were no threat, so this loss of communication was baffling. But then, investigators like Charleton and Meagen were not employed to think, just to react. They had been on the explorer craft as a protective force to the scientists and since being on Earth that role had become more one of baby sitter as the dangers and threats were minimal.

Finally they sighted the landmarks that were described to them as markers for the underground bunker. There was a sharp left hand turn in the sandy track and in line with that a small hill rose on the horizon, the bunker should be due north about one hundred yards. Following these directions they dismounted their bikes to search for the entrance, they knew they had to move around the sand to find a trapdoor. The area looked undisturbed so again the reason for the breakdown in communication remained a mystery. Finally Charleton felt the density under his feet change and realized he was standing on the trap door, together they bent down and moved the sand until the door appeared. Warily they lifted it and saw the ladder that would lead them to the control panel; one by one they embarked on the climb downwards. The ladder consisted of about twenty steps and as they neared the bottom the trap door above automatically snapped closed. Suddenly they were engulfed in darkness, and then after a short delay a light appeared to illuminate their path.

They stood at the base of the ladder and peered down a long tunnel, which glistened from the light shining off the minerals in the walls. It was almost magical, but the reason for their visit overwhelmed any sense of magic only mystery prevailed. Again the place looked undisturbed, not even footprints on the ground to mark any previous visitors.

"Do you not think it strange there are no footprints on the ground?" asked Meagen.

"A little," replied Charleton. "After all someone at some time had to come this way and there is no reason to cover your tracks unless you did not want anyone to be able to trace you."

"I think we need to proceed with extreme caution," she stated. "I am getting a very weird vibe from this."

"Vibe... what is that?" Charleton queried. "You sound more like these Earthlings every day. Have you got your Trispec with you, what does that say?"

"Stop being so scientific," persisted Meagen, "close your eyes and feel the vibrations around you, something is off here trust me."

"Just give me the readings and stop with that mumbo-jumbo please," he demanded.

"Alright... let me see. Okay the electro-magnetic reading shows recent activity here... I would guess about three people about four days ago, after that nothing. The readings do not look like Earthlings... in fact they have no real signature. They are not Cordite either," she replied puzzled. "I cannot make sense of this at all, the only thing I am sure of is that someone or something was here."

"Do you have the combination to the security panel?" Charleton asked as he tried to stay calm.

"It is in the machine I only have to press it against the panel to unlock the passage," she answered.

"Before you do... just examine the panel see if there are fingerprints or a machine imprint."

"No," she replied, "wiped clean as well... whoever did this is good. It is not easy to erase a machine imprint and leave no trace. According to my readings we are the first to ever unlock this panel... and I do mean EVER. All previous readings are gone completely." She pushed and prodded the spectrometer in an attempt to get a different reading.

"EVER... now that is what I call weird. I think we should go in armed, goodness knows what awaits us inside. Whatever this vibe thing of yours is, I think I am feeling it now too."

They both drew their weapons and Meagen pressed the Trispec against the panel to unlock the door. As they both held their breaths the door slid open.

Slowly they walked through the door and were presented with another door and another security panel.

"Were we briefed on a bi-secure system?" Meagen asked.

"Not to my recollection," he replied. "Let us just hope the code for this door has also been programmed into your Trispec."

Again Meagen pressed the Trispec against the panel and again the door slid open. This time they were presented with a dimly lit passageway with doors leading off it and at the end a large room beckoned them. Looking at each other they nodded in unison and proceeded guardedly down the passage, weapons drawn. After each step they paused to assess the situation. The silence of their surrounds was eerie, not a noise could be heard. There was no talking, no whirring of machines, no sound of work at all, the place was deserted, and again no sense of disturbance. It was like they were the first to set foot into this place, everything was pristine and new, unused.

As they entered the room they took different directions to assess the room; Meagen went left while Charleton went right. Circling the room they were struck by the many machines that now stood silent and the desks neatly stacked with papers that were empty. No sign of inhabitants or habitation was visible; no personal touches to the desks; not a thing out of place; it just was, it existed. They met in the middle of the room and looked at each other in disbelief. Charleton was the first to speak.

"Where is everyone? It is like they just disappeared..."

"Or never existed!" exclaimed Meagen.

"Maybe we should check all the rooms off the passageway before we make our evaluation," Charleton suggested.

"Let me get some readings from this room first," Meagen stated. "I want to see if whoever did this was as thorough here as they were in the passageway outside."

Adjusting the Trispec and scanning it around the room Meagen was engrossed in the readings she was receiving while Charleton inspected the desks more closely.

"These papers are neatly filed, no attempt to hide them or dispose of them... I wonder what they were working on?" he muttered almost to himself as he picked up a leaf of paper to read.

"Well there are no anomalies in these readings," Meagen stated. "They show three definite electro signatures and nothing more. I can see where they walked around the room, checked machines and sat at desks. There are no sudden movements, no struggles, everything is normal... maybe too normal."

"The information on these papers do not seem too top secret either, they simply state the conditions we found here when we arrived on this planet. Why this secret bunker for this?" he queried.

"Let us check out the other rooms before we report in," Meagen said as she began to walk into the long hallway.

"Good idea hopefully there will be more clues there," Charleton replied as he followed her out of the doorway.

As they opened the first door a light came on automatically to illuminate the contents of the room. It was obviously a living quarter with usual furniture, a bed, a wardrobe, a dresser and a desk; however what was missing were any personal touches; there were no photos, no computer, no clothes, it was bare.

Without a word the investigators moved onto the next room, they opened the door to the same picture and so on down the hallway. By the time they reached the final room they were more than a little spooked, by all appearances you would swear this place had never been inhabited.

"I do not get this... are we sure there were ever people sent here?" Charleton asked with a hint of frustration.

"According to HQ there are supposed to be three men here," she replied. "They were sent here over a year ago and their check-ins have been like clockwork till three days ago." She consulted her hand held computer digest as she spoke.

"Well where did they go and why did they go?"

"I suppose that is for us to find out."

"Okay where do we start?" Charleton asked.

"You go back and have another look at the papers in the main room," Meagen responded. "I will contact HQ and then have another look around. We have not found the kitchen or ablution area yet so I will keep looking, however I want us to stay in radio contact all the time, walk me through everything you do alright?"

Although they were partners Meagen had seniority and therefore took the lead on any investigation they undertook. At first this did cause a little conflict but now Charleton was used to it and respected Meagen for her abilities and leadership qualities. After all, he sometimes thought, any problems, she takes the fall, and he is left alone.

Using the wireless bud earpieces to communicate Charleton made his way back to the main room to have a closer inspection of all the papers neatly stacked on each desk. Meagen meanwhile reported their findings to HQ and set out their plan of action. Surprisingly, at least to her, HQ had no reaction to her news just agreed on her strategy and signed off.

"HQ did not seem surprised at our news... does that seem odd to you?" she asked Charleton.

"Odd describes this entire mission so far, I hope they will show a little more concern if we happen to disappear," he said with a laugh.

"I do not find that funny... how is your search going?"

"Nothing startling yet just a recount of our landing here and our findings upon arrival; I can see no reason why this research and this facility has been deemed top secret, all the information so far is readily available. My gut says there has to be more to this but I cannot locate it... I will keep looking though. How about you anything exciting?" Charleton said trying to keep his mood light.

"I have located the kitchen, it seems neat and tidy there is food here. The pantry and fridge are full, wait a minute... yes we have some food scraps in the bin. Obviously at some time someone has eaten here... it does not look too old, not moldy yet. The plates and cutlery however are all clean and neatly stacked away. Somebody sure did a great clean up job on this place all I can find is minimal electro signatures, I cannot even confirm if the signatures are the same person or their race. I have never seen anything like this... what the hell happened here?"

"I feel we have walked into a real life jigsaw puzzle, only half the pieces are missing. I guess we just keep looking... they – whoever they are – must have made one mistake, left one piece behind and we will find it," stated Charleton determinedly.

"I am moving on to find the ablutions, keep checking all the papers. Actually check the floor, under cupboards and chairs; there may be something that dropped and our mysterious 'friends' missed it," instructed Meagen.

"On it Boss," Charleton answered sarcastically.

"Do not call me that you know I hate it."

"Yes I do," he laughed.

Meagen made her way back up the hallway and around a corner and there was another door, she opened it slowly and found what she had been searching for. There was a row of sinks and mirrors, much more than needed for three men, maybe this facility was built to house more. Around another corner were the showers and toilets and again everything was spick and span, not what you would expect for three men alone. Along the left hand wall was a row of lockers with nametags attached to three of them. Finally some evidence that life did exist here at some time.

Meagen walked up to the first locker and inspected the nametag it was hand written in blue ink and read *'Roman North'.* She opened the locker door hoping to find Roman's belongings but alas it was not to be... it was bare and clean. The second locker belonged to *Oliver Point* and again all of his goods were missing as well. The final named locker was the *'property of Julius Search'* according to the tag on the door. Inside Meagen was surprised to see a piece of paper screwed up and shoved into a corner, without hesitation she bent down to pick it up, all the time giving a commentary on her ear piece to Charleton.

"What is written on the paper?" Charleton asked impatiently.

"Give me a minute I am trying to unscrew it without damaging it, I also need to scan it first to ensure I do not compromise any evidence left on it" replied Meagen with a similar degree of impatience for her partners attitude to due process.

"You are always so pedantic... have you ever done anything impulsively?" he enquired with a touch of sarcasm.

"Actually yes... I agreed to be partnered with you and look where that got me," she said with a laugh, trying to lighten the moment. "Okay I have a print and some DNA on the note, the Trispec is processing it... it will take a minute to scan all the data bases."

"Alright but what is written on the paper... is anything written on the paper?"

"I am getting to that, just be patient," she chided him.

"I am coming to you... hold on," Charleton announced as he ran to her location.

Charleton entered the bathroom and was met by Meagen's puzzled face.

"What is wrong... is there nothing on the paper?" he enquired

"Yes... but it make no sense to me," she replied as she handed him the note.

There written on the crumpled piece of paper were three words and some numbers... *'The Small Dragon... 124-13; 152-31'.*

"What is that supposed to mean?" he said, almost angry.

"I have no idea but it is obviously important otherwise there would have been no reason to leave it... perhaps it is a code?" she surmised.

"Code for what... and how are we supposed to decipher it... this assignment just gets weirder and weirder."

"Wait a minute the fingerprint and DNA is coming back... it belongs to... Dr Francis Brown... he apparently works at HQ in special projects he is an anatomical physicist. How would his fingerprint and DNA get here... unless... he worked here? Hang on let me check something," Meagen said as she busily typed into her computer digest.

"What are you thinking Meagen?" Charleton queried.

"Just a hunch... as I thought. The names on the lockers do not exist. I think they are part of the clue. Look at them individually then put all the surnames together," she suggested.

Charleton looked at the lockers and then slowly said the names out loud "North... Point... Search. Do you think whoever left this want us to search in a northerly direction... then what does the note mean?" he continued.

As she stared at the crumpled piece of paper in her hand Meagen also began to speak almost to herself; "if they want us to search in a northerly direction then maybe... the numbers could be... perhaps they are... co-ordinates and the small dragon is what we are looking for?" she asked more than stated.

"Makes about as much sense as anything else here today," stated Charleton.

"Let us make our way back to the surface and see what we can find," Meagen said, almost as if she were making the decision as she spoke it.

"Should we tell HQ what we plan?" he asked

"Let us just look to see what we find then we can brief them. After all I may be wrong this may be a wild goose chase," Meagen said totally unconvinced of her supposition.

They made their way to the surface and then input the numbers into the computer digest to see what result they would get. As they waited with bated breath and staring at the screen, many thoughts went through their minds... thoughts they were not comfortable in voicing. Eventually after what seemed like a lifetime but in reality may have been all of twenty seconds the screen started to form a map and the voice started issuing instructions.

"Move twenty paces to your right then turn forty-five degrees and proceed for two hundred meters," it said.

Both Charleton and Meagen looked at each other shrugged, then proceeded to follow the instructions.

Once they had completed these first instructions and stopped the computer voice spoke again. "Turn another fifty degrees to your left and proceed for ten meters and you will have arrived at your destination."

Again they followed the instructions, stopped and looked around. There was nothing.

"Do you see anything... something that does not belong perhaps?" Meagen asked Charleton more in hope than with knowing.

"Not really, all I see is sand and more sand... there is not even a tree or twig. Perhaps we have to dig... maybe it is underground just like the bunker," he stated, hoping to sound intelligent.

"That is not as silly as it may first sound... this is the place the numbers sent us so let us just start digging," Meagen replied rather resigned.

They both knelt down and starting removing sand from the spot they had been directed to. As fast as they removed the sand it appeared to replace itself and they were getting nowhere fast.

"I have an idea... why don't we have one of us to dig the other hold the sand back," suggested Charleton.

"Okay... I will dig and you can hold back because your hands are bigger and have more capacity to hold back than I do," she said

Within seconds of implementing this plan they saw progress, a hole started to develop in front of them, and shortly afterwards Meagen hit something.

"Wait I think I have found something... there is a solid article here. Just let me get a grasp of it and I will pull it out."

"This is just like a treasure hunt... how much fun is this?" Charleton said excitedly.

"Really Charleton... sometimes I wonder if you ever grew up," Meagen said. "I think I have it, it's a metal box." As she retrieved it from the ground and dusted all the sand off it she stopped dead and stared at the box in her hand. "Look at that," she said pointing to the lid of the box, "I think we have the right thing."

There on the lid was a transfer of a little dragon smiling up at them.

"Well that solves the riddle of the little dragon now let us see if we can solve the mystery of the disappearing scientists?" Charleton said sarcastically.

Slowly Meagen opened the box and found a paper file as well as a computer mini-drive, however on top was a single piece of paper folded and placed neatly into the box. She picked it up, unfolded it and began to read.

If this box has been retrieved it means we have failed and it is up to whoever is reading this note to ensure the information gets to the right people.

Please whoever you are DO NOT notify the authorities because it was orders from them that saw our demise and necessitated the use of this ruse.

Contained in this file and on this mini-disc is proof of our origins and the true story of what happened on Earth. It is imperative that this truth is exposed and to ensure those responsible are unveiled and this type of conspiracy NEVER occurs again.

From this moment on your life will be in peril but if you believe that truth must always triumph you will have the courage to see this mission through.

Contained in the file is the person to whom this information must be transmitted and they will ensure the dissemination of the truth. In the name of humanity I thank you for your courage to see this mission to its conclusion and if you cannot commit yourself to this cause I will understand BUT I plead with you not to destroy what you now hold but to pass it on to one who sees the value of placing the needs of the whole above the needs of the individual.

Meagen and Charleton stared at each other, each waiting for the other to say something, neither wanting to be the one to voice their opinion first.

"Meagen, we ARE the authorities," Charleton said with a quiver in his voice.

"We did nothing to these people and I do not believe our superiors did either. After all if they did why would

91

they then send us to investigate?" said Meagen sounding like she was attempting to convince herself more than Charleton. "However we do have a decision to make... do we report this or see the file gets to the right person?"

"When you say right person do you mean our superiors or the person nominated in the file?" queried Charleton.

"I am not sure... I think we need to read the file see what information it contains and then make our decision," she replied.

"The minute we open that file we put our own lives on the line... you do know that don't you?" Charleton suggested.

"I think we are past that point... the minute we were sent on this mission our lives became irrelevant. The only thing that matters now is if it is worth our lives... is the information contained in this file worthy of the sacrifice we are to make?... I for one would like that question answered."

"What do you mean our lives became irrelevant?"

"If these people thought this secret was worth killing for, and they are part of the authorities, they know we have been sent here. One and one always gives you two. If we are here we may or may not have found something, they cannot take that risk... we are irrelevant in the scheme of things and two more casualties is obviously nothing to these people," she concluded.

"Well then let's see what we are about to die for," he said matter-of-factly. "However I think we need to get back down into the bunker... we are sitting ducks up here."

With this point agreed they made their way back down but on the way rigged some make shift booby traps so they could be forewarned of intruders.

They decided not to investigate the mini-drive at the moment as inserting it into a computer may alert whomever they were now hiding from. On the same note they deleted all references to their search on the computer digest including the hidden back up and then burnt the note they found. Feeling comfortable that they had covered their tracks they felt it was now time to make a report to HQ. Trying to remain calm, Meagen reported their search had been fruitless and no sign of the scientists had been found, it was like they had just disappeared, she told them. There was also no sign of what they had been working on she told them. She then told HQ they would make one final sweep before returning and then signed off.

"That should cover us for the moment and give us time to decide what our next step should be," she said as she and Charleton settled down to see what the file contained.

They made themselves comfortable in the main room and together began to read over the file they had found. Silently they perused the words written in front of them, each lost in their own thoughts.

Once complete they sat and stared at each other, neither of them able to form a thought or a word. The information that has just been imparted to them was too astronomical to be true... it could not be what happened... no one could be that hard. They themselves were part of this conspiracy, unwilling and unknowing participants but participants nonetheless.

They had discovered that Earth's destruction had not been the result of a war but corporate greed. Big corporations had made contact with emissaries from Cordia and made plans to 'trade' with them. The destruction of Earth was their handiwork and they and their supporters lived in luxury in places untouched by the fall-out thanks to Cordia technology. The same technology could be used to regenerate Earth and reverse the effects on all life forms. The 'creatures' that now dwelt on these shores could be normal, could be 'human' again, they had to be made aware, made to care. Cordites also had to realize their part in this and take responsibility for the near eradication of an entire race and planet.

"This needs to be told to everyone and we need to fix this... we need to make it right..." Meagen muttered.

"Fix it... HOW... it is already done. However I agree we need to get this to the person named here and hope they can get the word out before they are eliminated as well," Charleton said with determination.

"Agreed this is our mission before they catch us and we become irrelevant; I want my death to be for the greater good and hopefully we will be the last to die in their attempt to keep this truth from the masses."

The two investigators made their way out of the bunker and to the surface, mounting their machines they were both filled with the anxiety that precedes an act of rebellion. They were determined in their actions and they knew their mission was just; they would make a difference. As they disappeared over the horizon the wind swirled the sand around the hatch that marked the entrance to the bunker, making it almost invisible. Invisible but not impotent... it had yielded its secret and the truth was already on a pathway that would lead it to the light.

At the beginning of this day these two investigators embarked on a mundane assignment but by day's end they had been recruited to ensure the world became aware of an enormous wrong and their own lives were now in the balance. This was the type of day we all hoped for, to be relevant to do something meaningful to ensure our life was not wasted, to right a great wrong, that we put the needs of the many before the needs of the few; a truly selfless act. Or on a smaller scale to put one person's needs before your own, to exercise your own humanity... just a little.

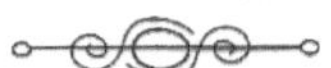

Concept idea given to authors to write story = Two investigators are sent to discover the cause behind a delay in a mysterious project.

Joyce P. Johnson is 59 years old and married for 38 years with two grown very successful children.

Her first published novel was 'Genesis of Memory', book one of the Genesis Saga. She is currently working on 'Genesis of Betrayal', which was preceded by 'Genesis of Life', 'Genesis of Destiny', and 'Genesis of Love', all of which will shortly be available. You can follow the progress of the Genesis Saga on its Facebook page 'Genesis of Memory'.

Joyce P. Johnson has been writing since she was eight years old. Writing for her was an escape, a refuge, a place she could imagine all types of wondrous things.

The Puppet Will Dance

BY KRIS SOLDBERG
AND
D.C. DAINES

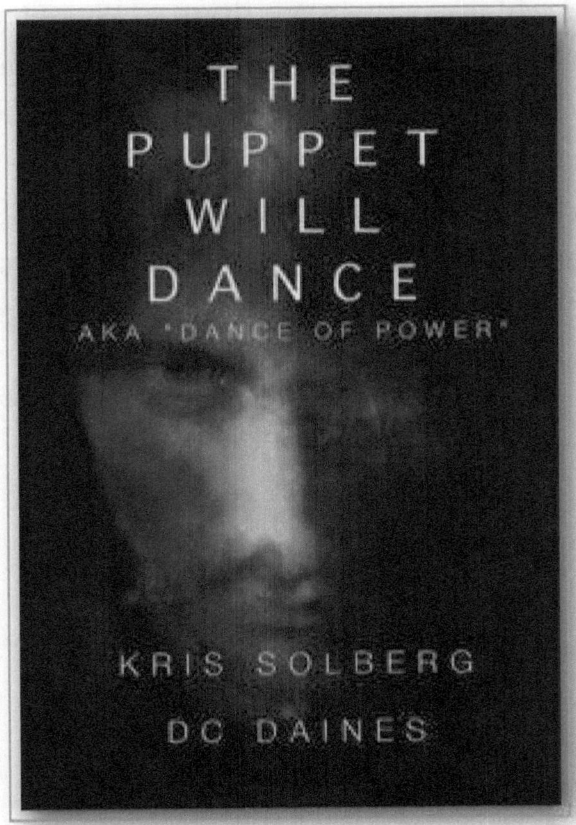

The shadows dance around the room; it's a slow, passionate dance between good and evil. The darkness throws itself over the light, with the bright gleam bravely fighting against the blackness' oppression. I'm lost in their movement.

"Why are you doing this?"

The voice cracks my dream, shatters my hopes. It throws off the dance.

"Please, just let us go."

Their whimpers push me down. Their silent weeps stack on top of me until I can't stand any longer. The weight is forcing me towards the cold soil of the Earth.

"What do you want from us?"

Want? They think I'm doing this because of my own desires, because I want to be here. They're wrong, they're all wrong. They'll soon see what I want, what I need, what I am going to get.

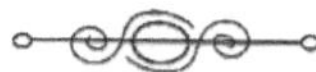

Click.

"Negotiator Rain?"

"Yes, it is I."

"I know you are off duty... spending time with your family, sir... but–"

"Get to it man. What is the matter?"

"We have a situation."

"Apart from your apparent lack of gumption?"

"Ah, sir?"

"And, you have no one to do my job whilst I am on leave?"

"We did sir."

"And?"

"He is dead!"

"That could be a problem."

"Yes sir."

"My family is out. I have a few hours before they are due to return. You can give me the address on the way Sergeant."

Click.

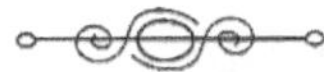

I hear the screams of the sirens, the screams of the children lying crumpled up against their parents, the screams of the dying security guard with a new-found hole in his head. His screams mock me the most.

Another scream shrieks through the room as the phone starts to ring. I don't want to talk to them, not now, not yet. I'm not ready. I need more time.

"Please, why won't you answer? Tell them what you want, so we can get the fuck out of here!"

They're getting restless. I don't like it when people yell at me.

The metal hugs affectionately against my skin as I pull the trigger. A middle aged man falls towards the ground with an indescribable scream. He joins in the chorus of the damned.

They're all mocking me.

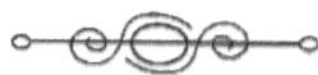

Why won't he answer the phone? What does he want? What will he demand? Well, he can't demand anything if he won't answer the damn phone.

"Sergeant?"

"Yes, negotiator Rain."

"Has he demanded anything yet?"

"No sir. We waited for you to make first contact."

"Rightly so. With the phone skills you possess you'd have given him a helicopter, fuel money and a burger before the end of the first conversation."

The boy standing before me stood defiantly at my comment yet his eyes told otherwise. You can tell a lot about a man from his eyes and his were those of a sheep. A law enforcement officer that took orders well, but had no feel for the real world. The world of the criminal. That is my world, seeing into the minds of depraved individuals. Men and women that take the lives of others into their own hands just because they had little to no life of their own, or they felt that the world owed them something. Well I owed this man something, and he was going to be collecting in spades. All he needed to work out was whether he wanted an open or a closed casket. Maybe I'd make that decision easy for him and unload my 44 into his face, the scum.

"Ah, sir?" I'd almost forgotten about the imbecile beside me, and the ringing phone, the sound of it being drowned out over the newly added sirens.

"Pick up the damn phone!" A blank look was still plastered across his face as I turned back to him.

"Sergeant, what happened to the other negotiator?" What, is this brain surgery? C'mon man, it was a simple enough question that I repeated again, emphasizing every syllable. "What happened to the other negotiator?"

"He-e-e was killed in his..." Bang. Was that a gunshot from inside, muffled by the obscene amount of noise now surrounding me?

"Shut off the sirens and shut your chattering. Do it now!" I barked as I looked through the mass of blue flashing lights, waiting for a barrage of hostages to exit through the front door... Nothing. The sirens started shutting down, first one and then another, then a Bang! This time it was clear. It was a gunshot; the screams that followed could be heard as well through the drone of the last few sirens. Ring, ring, ring...

"You could not be connected, please try again later and I am sure an operator will be here to help."

Click.

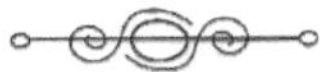

He's here. Finally, he's here. I have longed for this moment, yearned to see his tough facial tones, strived to hear his rugged, muscular voice. I see him through the dancing blinds; he's oozing authority, with every word thrown out of his lips with unquestionable legitimacy. The sirens have stopped their wailing, yet the ringing won't stop. I'm ready now.

"Hello? Who is this? Can you tell me how things are in there?" It's not him. W-why... won't he-e-he talk to me-e?

"Put him on. NOW!" My tone snarls with commanding authority yet my lips tremble as the line falls silent. Where is he? Why won't he talk to me? What have I done wrong? Come on, answer me. Answer ME!

"Yeah, wha'doya want?" It's him. My heart shakes, sending tremors through my chest.

"You know what I want" I beg my voice to stay firm, but it can't deliver "You know w-what I ne-eed"

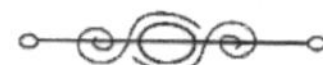

One last wail like a dying lady as the sirens finally stop, what has become of the hostages inside? Has he killed one? Two? Or were they just warning shots? The thoughts go through my head as I hand off the phone to the Sergeant, its ringing tone echoing in the receiver yet again.

"Don't speak!" I emphasize as I turn to the detective who now walks towards me, his long coat doing nothing to hide his arrogance. I wonder what they would do if I shot him in the face, would they pin a medal on me or just give me a raise?

"Rain." his tone was meant to insult, slime slithering off his tongue before biting into his cigar, the end easily demolished in those carnivorous teeth. Turning he spits, his aim perfect as it sticks to my boot. I do not respond, my boot staying planted. Oh how I'd like to plant my boot up—

"I said don't talk you imbecilic moron." My chin stays taught, a slight redness to my face at the Sergeant's obvious lack of phone etiquette, but I must remain in control. I reach for it, the receiver, looking through the rustling blinds, but there is nothing I can see. I am blind! Smoke wafts into my face as I hear the exhale from that jack-ass before me. I could...

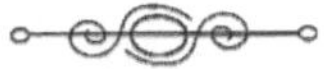

The bar is smoky. Too smoky, too many imbeciles for my liking but I look across the table and my wife and kids laugh heartily at the idiot up on the stage. There is something not quite right about him, I can feel it, my skin crawls and my arm hair is raised yet he is entertaining my family. If he is doing it, then I don't have to waste my energy trying to please them. I can handle a little discomfort if it allows me some reprieve from their constant nagging. I bury myself in another drink, lifting my head to see that they are all pointing at me. What the... I am up on stage. He has a watch. Crappy old thing it is. He talks like a mad man. "Sleepy...", yeah right. "Look into...", ha ha, what a joker.

"ANSWER ME!" the shouting down the receiver breaks me from the trance. What happened? That has never happened before. I act quickly, my words neither thought out or witty. "Yeah, wha'doya want?" Oh my god, did I really just say that?

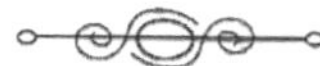

My fingers cradle the receiver, nurturing it as I hold it in my hands. I see him through the blinds. He's angry, angry at his co-workers, at himself but... not at me, never at me.

"Do you recognize my voice?" My tone is eager, begging for a response, for a confirmation. He has to remember, he has to.

"Nah, should I?" It can't be. How can he not remember me? It's impossible. The mere notion is... that's IM-impossible!

"Y-ye-yeah. You-u s-sh-sho-should". Relax, calm down. Don't embarrass yourself. Regain control.

"Well, I don't. You wanna refresh my memory?" Take control. He's at your mercy, MY mercy.

"I'm the reason you're here, the reason you're standing in the cold evening air as oppose to sitting snuggled up next to your family." I hear his heart skip a beat. The mere mentioning of his family makes him putty in my hands. He's under my control now. "Speaking of, where is your family? Where is your wife and daughter?"

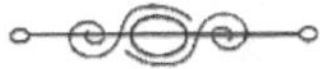

My head is spinning, the smoke has returned, the dumb-ass detective before me is still breathing out that filth. There is something familiar about the voice on the other end of the line, but I just can't place it. The smoke, the situation, all too familiar, yet out of reach. Why? He asks me questions like we are long lost friends. Companions from another time. I am starting to lose it, my frustration with the imbeciles around me showing as the stupid Sergeant starts to speak while I am trying to listen.

A quick flick to his ear lobe, a stinging glance and he falls silent again. I can see the situation before me clearly... No I can't! If this dick does not stop breathing his filth into my face I am going to...

Calm. Think calm thoughts, calmness that is contagious. He is playing with me, he is the reason I am here? I am the reason he won't be here. In time. In time he will get what is coming to him, he will be ended like this pointless heist of his. He will be ended and I will be at home with my family and their monotonous boredom. MY FAMILY! What does he know of them? Why would he be asking? I put my hand over the receiver, speaking to the moron detective before me.

"Get me my family! Get hold of them now!" He stammers, his mouth moving but nothing coming out except that disgusting smoke. I should... no, control.

"Please." Oh, the pain of that last word as I remove my hand from the mouthpiece. "My family? Now what would you know about that?"

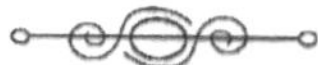

"I know more than you'd ever believe"

"Is that so? Enlighten me." His voice reeks of arrogance but his tone betrays him. He's terrified of what I might say next, of what I might know. He's terrified of me.

"I know that your wife has a scar running along her elbow from when she broke her arm two years ago. I know that your daughter has an imaginary friend named Stuart, who's an unemployed plumber." The other end is quiet, filling our conversation with deadly silence. I am in charge, and he knows it.

"But most importantly, Investigator Rain, is that I know your daughter, at this very moment, is trying to shake new life into her mother, bleeding to death on the floor in front of me."

I hear his wheels turning, his cells churning. He doesn't know what to think any more, he doesn't want to believe me but... right about... now he is realizing he doesn't have any other choice.

"I don't believe you." Lies, all lies.

"Your words might be secure, but your voice is betraying you." Putty in my hands. He's putty in my hands.

Silence floods the room as he throws the phone away. His emotions are gaining control, slowly tearing away at his exterior persona. Let the madness consume you, Rain, you'll enjoy it.

Eyes stare back at me as I gaze around the room. They're filled with dread, fear and anxiety.

"Please, help my mommy" It's a kind, nourishing little voice that stares up at me with unbridled purity. I bury my eyes in hers. She reeks... of hope and innocence. Time to change that.

The metal dangles lightly in my fingers, eagerly begging to be set free once more. It knows what is about to happen.

"Absolutely, little girl. I'll help your mommy!"

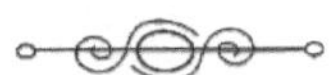

My daughter is inside! My Daughter is inside! My DAUGHTER IS inside! MY DAUGHTER IS INSIDE! The thoughts beat within my head, his words bouncing around my skull as hornets from a disturbed nest. What had happened? Why had it happened? Who was this man? What was this man? What did he want with me? What did he want with my family? No. No. Nooooooo!

"Rain, I can't get hold of your family." He talks as though it is a shopping errand. As though I have asked him to go to the market and get me some toilet paper. That obnoxious fuck. The gall of this pompous prick standing before me while my family is inside, my wife dying, my child scared half to death.

"Give me your phone", I shout, my hand outstretched. He complies as he puffs out another of his smoke animals. The beast within the smoke attacks my eyes, they burn, tears forming as I claw back my sanity, yet something is there in the back of my mind. A voice, the voice from the phone. The voice from last night. It is saying to me. "Kill," images flash across my mind, ones of the joker on the stage the night before, the hypnotist. His whispers in my ear "Kill the negotiator." His hand kindly grips my shoulder as he replies as if talking to himself.

"Why, why do you need me to kill the negotiator?" Replying to his own words he continues, that devilry grin across his face. "I need a formidable opponent for my masterpiece of course, why would there be another?" Images flash again, the Negotiator, my friend of 20 years, his door opening and his smile, a gentle hand upon my shoulder and then...

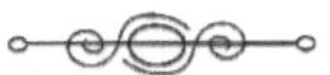

Blood, blood and teeth respond violently as I smash the receiver into the detective's jaw. He drops to the ground instantly, his jaw, glass and his mind shattered. "Get me his Kevlar coat, his firearm and his shotgun," the Sergeant is standing there with his jaw dropped, the saliva drooling from his open mouth. Slap, his senses return with the red lash of my open hand.

He tries to talk but I silence him with a finger to my mouth as I dial on the detective's phone, my own phone lying smashed upon the pavement. Ringing, the phone is ringing, no gunshot yet, maybe I have time. "Sergeant?" he looks at me with a dumb glare, I think of putting him down, of silencing his ridiculous mind however I am in need of his assistance. "Where did the negotiator die?"

I already know the answer, his babbling not even reaching my ears as I put on the detective's coat, loading the gun and shotgun into it. Handing the Sergeant my coat I continued. "Ah, I see you answered. So you know how to use a phone. Shoot a lady and hypnotize a Negotiator." silence, I had struck a nerve. He had the upper hand and he knew it. Maybe I could use this to my advantage.

"I seriously have no concern for my wife. The minute she gets out of this predicament she will nag me to death with concerns over why I got her out and not my daughter. So I tell you this, my daughter for the asshole detective I have at my feet. Yes, he got in my way. He is no longer in my way. Don't make the same mistake! So I make this proposal, give me my daughter, you get a Detective as a hostage and you can keep my wife. Deal?" The silence was golden. His heart beating faster, I could hear, yet his voice, outside my head I could not. Kill, kill, kill. His voice inside my head returned as I looked across at the Sergeant, my coat still dangling from his outstretched arm, clinking, his eyes registering what I wanted him to do as I reach into the coats pockets and remove...

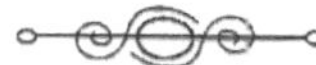

The wailing is back, the screaming has returned. My demons are waiting at the crevice of my sanity. His words are gaining confidence, yet I can't tell if his voice is sincere. He wants me to keep his wife, he doesn't care. He's playing me, I know he is, but I can't prove it. I have become a pawn in his game, I must regain my control.

"Still there, funny man?" What do I say? How do I crawl my way back to the top?

"You can't ha-ha-v-ve her... I-I..." Wake up, liven up. Pull yourself together! "You can have the other one, the damaged one, the dying one."

"And... you'll accept the detective in exchange?" That tone, it's insecure, nervous, anxious. I have him, I fooled him. He's mine again.

"Yes, I will accept your detective, although he doesn't look too be doing so well."

"Think of it as one damaged individual in exchange for another."

My gun is pointed towards the chorus of the doomed, the metal clunks as it glides out of its socket. The blood weeps out of the cavity I have created.

"Wha-what was that? Why are you shooting in there?" That tone, I bathe in his neurosis.

"You only said you wanted her back, you never said in what capacity." I am in control, he's my pawn and I am his king. Bow down to me! "I'm ready to make the exchange now."

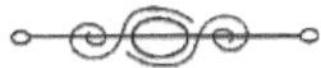

Writhing anger, pain, the player was played. She will be nothing but a BLOODY CORPSE. Oh well, better than my daughter. Wives are replaceable, but your child is part of you, and I bet that is what the gunman inside was counting on. I had jumped the gun and paid the price. My face pulsed as the swelling took hold. I had him wrong, that Sergeant. He had some balls after all, and some right hook reinforced by the butt of his gun. Spitting blood to the side I hobbled towards the entrance. It also seems I underestimated the Detective, as he regained consciousness before I was ready, then put one straight in my leg for my indiscretion.

The trail of blood behind me added to my deception as I made my way to the entrance, the Sergeant beside me shitting himself. I chuckled to myself, his balls seemed to have shriveled again. This was going to be one bloody ending and I knew it. Fumbling with the knives I had placed in my coat pocket I could feel their cold steel. Their coldness reminded me of what my wife's body would soon be; now her life was ended. That voice, no longer on the phone, cold, calculative, a monster's. He knew what he was doing, had planned this for months, even years. Why?

What had I done to deserve this? My job? Maybe it was my winning personality. His voice beat inside my head again, "Kill, Kill, Kill." No matter, he was going to get what he wanted. I was going to kill, kill and kill the son of a bitch inside, if it was the last thing I did.

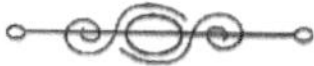

The door slides open, the light chases the darkness to the corners of the room. The screaming has stopped, silence has engulfed my being. His figure appears in the doorway, a dark, blood soaked man hobbles past the threshold; the threshold of rules, of law, of sanity. From here, it's all up to the individual, it all comes down to who wants it the most. "You don't fool me, Investigator. You can drop the charade, I know it's you"

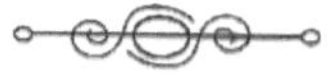

"Well that makes one of us, doesn't it? You know who I am, but I don't, not any more. The person I was before tonight is gone. The person I strived to become will never see the light of day. You wanted to push me over the edge, well... I hope you're ready to come flying with me"

His reply baffles me, why is he not under my control? The hypnotizing should have held. He should be putty in my hands. Arms soar out of his coat, three sharp, gleaming blades in each hand. They come flying towards me. I swerve out of the way but soon come to realize I wasn't fast enough. I-I'm bleeding, dying. My chest weeps, my body cries, my skin moans.

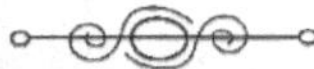

"This ends tonight, this ends now." My tone snarls out into the bright light behind him as I spew blood across the room. He's no longer a man, merely a shadow lining the walls of the entryway. I focus my eyes on the little girl, the little girl looking puzzled up at the bleeding man who is now in front of her, the man who used to be her father.

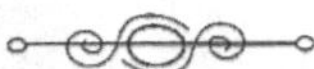

I point my gun in her direction, another knife soars towards me, and darkness covers my vision. I see his coat lying on top of the little girl, I feel the knife embedded in my neck. My blood is evacuating my body, my ship is sinking, but I won't go down alone.

My gun roars through the room with glee and excitement. It pounds into the coat with ferocious commitment. The girl will die, just like me...

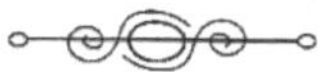

I stand at the threshold to the bank, pausing as I ready myself for what must be done. I know it must be done, the loss of a life so another can survive. A parentless child is better than one of no life. I have made arrangements, she will be cared for. I know after today that I will not survive, her needs greater than my own. What this man has made me into. This madman. He made me a killer, a sadist, him! I never thought of the glass as being half full but as half empty and now was no different. This glass needed to be emptied and I was the one to do it. I know it is the end as the door slides open!

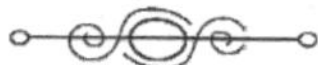

He makes me as I enter, he is smarter than I give him credit for. No matter, I am here, it is time to become what I strove to destroy. Swift and strong I fly in, my blades making their marks as he yelps like a wounded dog. His life is failing but not before he takes others.

They scream, they get up, they fall down. I can do nothing for them, these sheep to the slaughter. But I can to my daughter. My coat comes off, around her life, its

Kevlar coating stopping the death bullets. I hear her screams, sense her pain.

I feel her pain too as I fling the last of my knives, flicking it into his neck. His life will be over soon, my life too as many a stray bullet catches me. I must find out why he has done this, why he has taken these lives. I step forward as he drops to one knee, his gun raised at me. His eyes are crazed, my life, his life gone, he knows it, I know it.

Those eyes, so familiar to me, but why? The gun lowers as I stumble forward. My hand grabs at his throat, throttling him hard, yet my strength is failing. Looking deep in his eyes I ask, "WHY?" His only reply, his last breath, his only word; "Brother," as we slump to meet again in hell.

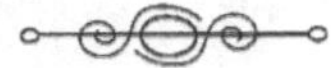

D.C. Daines resides in Western Australia and is the author of The Star Crystal.

Kris Soldberg is an Author with a passion for exploring the dark corners of his mind through writing.

Echoes

BY STEPHEN LANDRY
AND D.C. DAINES

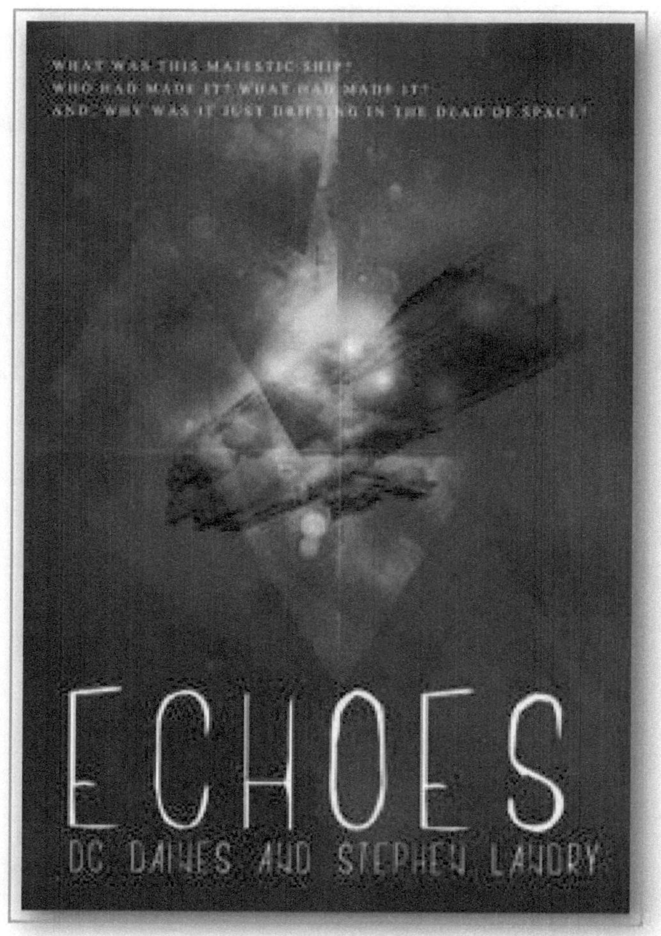

Ever since the first distress call, 20 years ago, I have been studying these creatures... I am not sure why, maybe it is the distance, my persistence, but now, only now have I been able to break their surface thoughts and delve deeper into their minds to see more of the picture and try to piece together the events as they have transpired. In such, I am hoping to devise a plan to stop the inevitable actions, the recurring cycle of these savages, The constant link to our brethren's fate has made us bitter, so I have, at greater loss, severed myself from them, But I cannot lose hope. I cannot give up. I must prevail. Their primitive minds are complicated, fractured, and my method sporadic, but we are close. Close enough for me to piece together the last few days, the hours, so when we reach our wives, husbands, children, we can save them. Save them without losing... losing ourselves...

In the last few hours, my methods have proven less effective than I had hoped, the savages attacking our sister ship seem to have broken the cycle, stopped the time loops that allowed me the time to study and tap into their minds. Now they are moving in real time, their lives on a collision course for ours. Yet through this I have found two glimmers of hope. One I have been prodding for years, but the other is new, less rigid, and very open to me.

But alas, I must work my way through their lives to get to the point that we are at now, I hope I will not be too late, with the events unfolding before I get to intervene. I must concentrate, put myself into their memories, their thoughts. The first is fractured, the deep sleep has broken his mind, he knows not of what he has done before or what he will do again, I hope we are not too late to save this one, the one that calls himself Bines.

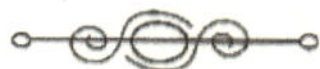

The cold vacuum of space called out to us like a mother calling for her lost child. Does it weep for us knowing we are so far from home? I opened my eyes for what felt like the first time. The gray walls were a blur. The cold liquid that surrounded my naked flesh turned to vapor. Slowly the air around me began to warm, like I was born for the first time; a child drawn into the light. I adjusted my posture, coughing up the last of the liquid that had engulfed my lungs. It tasted like spoiled milk. Lights appeared in front of me, projected on the glass. At first it seemed so strange. Small vibrant blue symbols appeared in lines one at a time. A few seconds passed, and as the symbols became more and more clear, I began to read them. Moments before it had all seemed so strange. The first was a question; "Rank?" The letters were blinking to grab my attention. The second was "Name?" The third, "Mission?" Each word layered one above the other like a list. Rank was the only one blinking. Slowly, I exhaled, and as I moved my tongue I felt the numbness inside my jaw fade away.

"Corporal Bines, salvage."

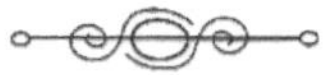

Bines's mind is hard to read at this time, their words are still foreign to me and his thoughts are trying to find themselves. Why have they not yet learnt to talk with their minds as we have done so for thousands of years? I am sure another opportunity will arise to... no matter, another snippet, no matter how small it may lead us to our salvation.

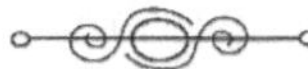

"Tell me something corporal, are you a religious man?"

The Captain, whom we called Commander, sat back in his chair. His eyes were glazed over. Mine were probably not any better. We had been in deep sleep for months and had only awoken a few hours earlier.

Before I could even remember everything about who I was, I had been called to his quarters. The walls had guided me to his quarters with small phosphorescent lights from the stasis chamber.

His mind became clearer from this point, recalling the history of his people and the one they call Bines. I am curious, he still chooses to blank out the other time-lines he has entered, I hope with all my strength; he remembers them and their outcome before it is too late.

On my way, my mind had filled in the blanks. Our ship was called the Geras. It was once the top of its class, built to explore the asteroid belt, and defend various mining and deep space operations. Soon though, lighter and faster ships had replaced it. All it was good for now was deep space salvage. It was supposed to be retired, and for all intents and purposes it was. As far as anyone would be concerned, we were flying a ghost. The sad part about that was that we had gone farther now than any human vessel in history, and no one would ever know. The radiation outside would have sunk through the hull of any other ship and killed the crew, but the Geras was thick and stubborn. It had been retrofitted with several new experimental ion drives that thrust us into the darkness. It was dark, dirty and rough, exactly the way we liked it.

"Tell me something corporal, are you a religious man?"

I stared at the Commander, brow raised in question. Had he already asked me this? He looked confused as well. "I don't know," I said, had I already said that?

For the duration of this voyage he was the only God I had. I answered with just that. Aside from myself, our crew was small. We only had a few dozen men and women, most with the same black ops training as mine. Others on board included biologists and lab techs with varying degrees. On paper none of us existed, no wives, no kids, and no families, aside from a few bastard children here and there. Living on the line was our life. If this mission went wrong in any way, only a few Generals and politicians would know, and they could drink it away.

I saluted and left, Or did I? How long now have we waited? Our section of space was nothing compared to the vastness of it all. Here on the edge of our solar system floated a derelict object of unknown origin. For so long we have been alone trapped in our little corner of space. This discovery was a means to an end.

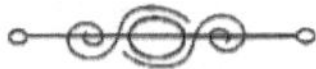

I find it of disturbing in nature that no family are present on the vessel. Is this why they are so quick to use violence, the reason they have no sense of life preservation? No matter, no time to ponder as the other one's emotions are stronger now. My... now I know why I have not felt his presence before this day, why his mind has not been accessible. The minds crowd mine, and pull at my consciousness. They show no respect, yelling at me, questioning my intrusion, but they are familiar to each other. Unlike the other vessel, they are family. This is something that must be exploited. The others fade as I grasp this thread, Clark's thoughts becoming one with my own as I enter his head. He is less fractured, clear are his thoughts, though his thoughts scare me, scare him.

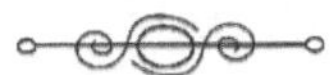

The saliva dripping from my open jaw hit the console with a hiss as I stood gob smacked. Without removing my gaze from the monitor before us, I slammed my fist down, the slight whirring sound signifying the cooling fan had started again. The normally rowdy crew were deadly quiet, their breathing drowned out by the hum of the drive engines as they powered down after the two hundred hour flight they had just endured.

What was this majestic ship in the monitor before us? I thought to myself, *Who had made it? What had made it? And, why was it just drifting in the dead of space?*

"When you have finished drooling all over my ship, Clark, then maybe you should try communications with that thing."

I had not heard the door behind me open, the slight quirky click as it jammed for a second, before releasing, nor had I heard the Ships Captain's footsteps behind me, or for that matter, seen his hand upon my console. The sight before me was that awesome. But now, as he reminded me of my duties, some of that awe left me. It was my job to communicate with it, to see if there was anyone aboard. To help the crew to get on the vessel without harm, and my job to decipher the command codes so we could... so we could gut her like a feral animal, a piece of garbage on the rubbish heap. *Please, not to her, she was just too beautiful.*

"Well man?" His gruff, I-have-not-got-a-minute-to-wait attitude rubbed me wrong. "What are you waiting for?"

Waiting, I thought to myself, *waiting for the ship to blow us out of our misery, waiting for the majestic beast before us to open fire and obliterate our sorry excuse of an existence. Waiting for... well, they were all waiting for me.*

"Yes Captain."

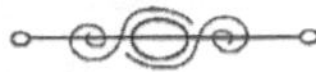

There may be hope for this one yet, his thoughts meld with mine as though we are one and he has felt our touch before. Maybe he has; we have reached out many times before without conflict. So why attack us now? No matter, Bines has returned and so have the headaches. The pills keep the pain away a little, but none mask the long-term effects of what I am doing. The blood flows freely from my nose.

"I know," I think aloud to myself, "this is why it is forbidden to meld with another species mind so completely. No matter, my resulting death is of no concern."

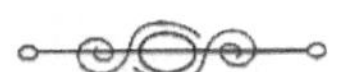

They had called all of us to the deck. Something was wrong. Each of us had been in bad situations before, and that feeling of dread, that feeling someone was about to attack, had become second nature. It was dizziness; a faint feeling in the air, like the oxygen around you had been lit by some kind of unnatural phenomenon.

It had been twelve hours since we woke up, but only eleven since we began our scans. There was nothing. No matter how many tests we ran the object seemed to be nothing more than an illusion. Hell, the only reason we knew it was here was because some amateur sighted it from a telescope and ran his mouth all over the wire. It was easy to cover up. Nobody was really interested in this sort of thing anymore. Unidentified Flying Objects? It was a joke. Even now, right here where we could physically see it out the viewport, we still didn't know if it were real. It was beginning to feel like we had traveled millions of miles for nothing more than a mirage.

Abruptly, the ship shook. It was like someone had launched a blast of energy at the Geras, and the impact caused the hull to buckle. The object didn't move but the sensors picked up another signature. It was a small blip, but it was more than enough for us to identify it. It was a human ship, and we weren't the only ones here.

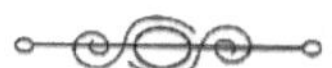

Pain continued to fill my senses, the drugs no longer helping to dull it. Yet at least there is another piece of the puzzle placed before me, this was the cause if my pain, the attacking of our sister ship, and by... Clark? His emotions flooded out, his disgust. It had been mere hours since I had first felt the pain and now I was privy to the reason for it, this was good. This immense feeling of emotion meant our minds are coming together, soon we would meet at the same point.

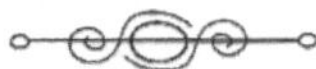

"Frigit, do you have to keep shooting at her? All you are doing is annoying her and corrupting my scans."

"Ah, Clark." Frigit's voice was strained, but no more than normal, she really did have a way of annoying me, but then, apprentices usually did.

"Ah, oscillating field... should be able to match the shields of the shuttle to allow us access. Are you listening Fr—?" My question was cut short. She had made her way over to me, tapped on my shoulder and was pointing at the big ass military vessel sitting above us, a model I had not seen since my apprenticeship. "Oh fuck!"

My ear stung as the Captain pulled at my ear lobe, dragging me along. "You're with me Clark. I have no interest in letting these folk get hold of my bounty, and because you took so long ogling that thing, you are going to make sure that they don't."

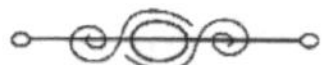

Curious, they both want our sister ship, do they know we are aboard, that our brethren live there? Or is the arrogance of their race that everything must belong to them? Bines is back.

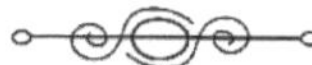

"God damn salvagers," the Captain said. "How did they even get all the way out here?"

It seemed impossible that here on the edge of the solar system were two human ships, both claiming the object as their own.

"How long have they been below us?" was the first question we had asked. They had seemed to come out of nowhere. Our ship dwarfed theirs, which brought us to our second question; "What type of ship is that?"

It seemed more exotic than most. It was small, like the newer ships that were being built close to home, and yet it looked completely different. Rather than a large or small rectangular block with tethers, cannon mounts and antenna that ran down the top of the ship like a spinal chord, the small ship seemed aerodynamic. It looked like it could just as easily fly on Earth as it could in space... yet it was just big enough for salvage. Perhaps a private company built it. For all we knew our mission had been scrubbed and something more experimental had been created during our sleep. For all we knew, we might have slept a lot longer than we intended. There was only one way we could know anything for sure, but when our comm officer, Grey, sent them verification codes, there was no response. Had we been less curious, we would have shot them out of the sky for not responding... which, coincidentally, was the Commander's first response. Fortunately, before that happened, they'd contacted us and requested a meeting to discuss an important matter.

Several hours passed before I approached the Commander. I still couldn't believe he considered blowing them out of the sky. They were harmless. If anything we needed them. They were calling the object their "bounty". Apparently they had managed to pull a few readings off it and map the outside. One of their crew, a man named Clark, had passed the data to us. It was more or less exactly what we were looking for. On the lower backside of the alien object there was an opening that looked enough like a hatch that there was nothing else it could be. Even if it was nothing more than a trash chute, it was still a way in; not to mention if it were a trash chute we would probably learn immensely more about them. Even if we couldn't knock or open the door we had the tools to drill inside.

The Commander finally agreed. We would allow some of their crew onto our bridge and using their resources first we could investigate the ship. In return we would pay them to scavenge the ship for us. It had become a win-win.

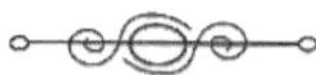

The thoughts crashed my skull, knocking Bines completely out of my mind, my eyes watering as Clark's emotions got the better of him again. Our link is growing stronger; this would be great if I knew that I was going to live long enough to get the chance to use it. For now, I find myself in Clark's memories hours later, yet only seconds have passed.

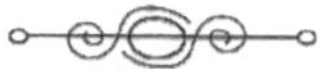

"No!" I screamed out "No, Nooo!" I turned to the Captain, finding him standing beside me on this foreign bridge. "Who sent the shuttle without my final tests, my results?! Who made the call to send my shuttle, my guys, to get onto... the ship? Who sent them to their deaths? Who the fuck did that?" The sight before me was horrific, the shuttle, our shuttle, had tried to enter through the force field, it had got inside. Then it disintegrated. I can only assume Frank and Bill were on board, but now they floated inside the shield, their bodies naked and lifeless.

"Seems that apprentice of yours is not as good as you. Pity, she was promising. I am sure you can, work out what she did wrong. Train her better. After all, you ain't g'tting any younger. You will need to retire soon enough." I turned, disgust in my face, my tone almost certainly going to continue screaming as I told him to— Part of the vessel opened as the bodies collided with it, swallowing them whole.

"Ouch!" The pain startled me as I swung around, ready to tear everyone a new hole after I was injected. My deathly glare turned the room quiet as my eyes were torn from the pointless death before me. "What the fuck?!"

"Just an inoculation sir," The medic's voice held firm as he callously returned the medical injector to its pouch. No wonder it hurt, it was a relic. Seeing my bewildered look at the item he smiled "we do not know what could be on that vessel." Friggin' military and their inoculations. *Damn them. Damn my Captain! "Damn! What did you say? On that vessel." My heart sank as I realized the ramifications, we weren't going to let a few deaths stop us from gutting the vessel like a fish.*

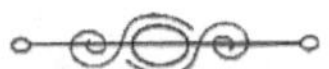

The minds are becoming one, they're merging as though they are deliberately combining with each other. Ah, I was mistaken, I thought they were more advanced than I originally surmised; instead it is obvious; they are physically close to one another. This will help my bond as Bines reacts to the proximity of Clark.

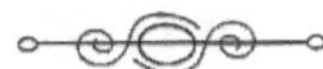

I could hear one of their crew screaming. He was just as sick about what the Commander did as I was, but on this ship the Commander is God. Once we knew there was a force field, it was only a matter of gearing up the right energy signature and blasting our way through it. It was only a temporary measure but once we were inside we could disable the shields from there.

I conducted the briefing. Once we penetrated the shield, our two teams – one from our vessel and one from theirs – would immediately embark. It was my job to lead my men into the unknown. The rush of it all made me feel like a child again, exploring the outdoors for the first time, wandering farther and farther into the woods. We had no idea what was waiting on the other side of that hatch. The only thing we could do was try and be prepared. The inoculations our chemists delivered hurt like hell, but were worth it. Small nanites would keep our blood from bursting out of our bodies should the pressure drop dramatically. They would also fight any alien contagions we might come across.

Our Commander had a strange look in his eyes as we left. I had that feeling again. Something seemed wrong and out of place. I began to double-check my gear. The spacesuit was like medieval armor, only instead of swords we carried rifles that we printed on the Geras. Both suits and weapons were made from carbon and metal alloy. The suits were lighter and more agile than those of the 21st century, and they had a HUD inside the visor that constantly fed us information about our surroundings. The rifles had thousands of small fibers at the tip that, with the press of a trigger, would ignite and project an energy pulse that could rip a torso apart. If the fibers were to overheat, the guns had a secondary weapon that would fire small metal projectiles that could shear through the hull on lightweight ships. Chances were we wouldn't need our guns, but we were soldiers first and we were prepared for anything. Death, terror, destruction, rescue, it didn't matter; this was what we were best at.

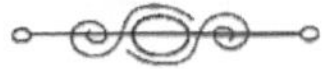

The weight of the joining struck me, blackness creeping into my mind as Bines continued to describe his weapons. In his eyes, they were an end to a cause, or a needed necessity in case of attack. But my brethren would not attack, we would not cause pain to others, or would we? I had disconnected myself from the others for too long. I mourned my loneliness and longed to again be reunited with them once more. Just once before my demise. For a moment I will let in in my own memories.

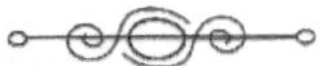

The object was immense. It dwarfed even the Geras. It took us over an hour for our shuttle to reach the hatch. The Geras sent out a pulse disabling the shield as we reached it. Each of us held our breath as we passed the threshold. Our bodies tensed. No armor would protect us if we got the math wrong. We were lucky. We passed and in moments we had begun drilling into the hatch.

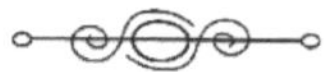

Siren like screams from my within our ship stirred me from my partial slumber, they were all screaming in unison. No, I was wrong, the ship was screaming out with its sister. They were doing something to her! They were hurting her! I must do something; I must stop Bines!

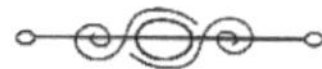

I was one of the first to step inside. With the shields disabled we were able to take a pretty good scan of the interior. The atmosphere was breathable, and the helmets were a hindrance, so I called in a sit-rep and advised we were leaving our helmets in the shuttle. Ops control acknowledged and advised us to proceed with due caution. The dark empty corridors were lifeless and stale. The walls were solid black, although there was something familiar about them. I had a sense of déjà vu as we walked further and further inside. We used the lights at the end of our rifles to pierce the darkness around us. The rooms began to open up. The HUD that would have appeared on the visor now appeared on my wrist, feeding me intel and displaying a map as we walked slowly through the alien architecture. Everything and everyone was silent. The only sound we heard were our own footsteps and the occasional creak, as if the hull were shifting like an old house in winter, as we came closer and closer to the place where we believed we could control the shields.

We walked slowly inside a huge room that must have acted as a bridge or control center. The HUD on my wrist was feeding me more and more information about the room and the alien ship. We were a hundred percent certain now that we were on-board a star-ship. It was ancient. The walls were no longer solid black, but instead they were now grooved and engraved with symbols that I could not recognize. I stared, believing that they would come into focus the way the symbols came into focus when I woke from stasis. Nothing happened; the symbols remained illegible. It still didn't stop any of us from staring. Clark, one of the smartest from the other vessels crew, had figured out how to disengage the shields. Not moments after he had done so, the Commander himself pronounced he was coming on board with another squad. We were told to sit and wait.

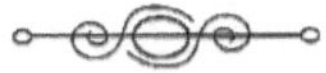

Am I too late, have they already sealed our fate? Will my brethren be sanctioned to death because I could not complete this task I have set myself? Wait... we are close, so close I can feel my family. They mourn for me, the separation I have forced upon them, but it was necessary, to break the link to create another. They are no longer in

the time loop and they can see the carnage, feel all the time lines rush into one as they collide. I will keep trying, stopping Bines and his team is my goal, my brethren's will be stopping the destruction of our sister's life as she calls out. However, once before my demise, I want to reach my family again.

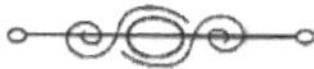

I thought for a moment I had heard a little girl's voice, but there was nothing. The silence was maddening. Every time someone would try and say something someone else would think they heard something strange. In the darkness it seemed like the minutes had become hours, and maybe they had.

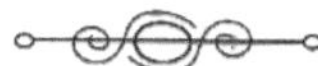

Voices, voices in their heads, I must stop them before the killing starts again. The other time-lines all ended badly, but not this one; this one must end better as I am here, and with the temporal distortion destroyed by the presence of the second vessel, I have no choice; there are no more second chances. I have broken through; I am now in the same time line, the same thought. I am using Bines to amplify my will, using my thoughts to infect fear into the others.

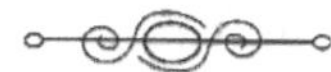

Abruptly, communication with the Geras ceased. The HUD on my wrist disappears. Only the light from our rifles remains, but now the room and hallways around us light up softly, much the way a subway tunnel or terminal would be lit. My heart is racing. I can feel the nanites burning inside my veins as they fight back hard against something that doesn't belong. I feel like my whole body is on fire and for several seconds my mind imagines that it is. One of my men, the shuttle pilot named Jason, starts screaming. He begins to cry.

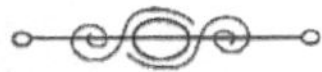

Fractured, thoughts have become hard to read, the emotions destroying my mind as I scream out in pain, the pain must stop, no, the throbbing. I cannot take it any more; I have failed. Blood pours from my eyes, the tears burning my flesh as I lose control, the one I am connected to screams, he knows I am in his head, fights to push me out, yet instead he...

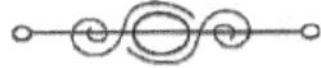

I give the order for everyone to return to the shuttle. I lean to grab Jason, who has fallen to his knees. He is still crying, begging for his life. Before I can disarm him, he unloads a single energy pulse inside his mouth, tasting the carbon fibers that burn and incinerate what was once his skull.

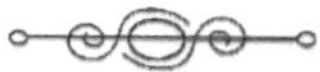

Noooooooooo!

Now it is up to them, the weapon fire causing the ship to use protection mode, they are doomed and I have failed. My knees give me no comfort as I rock back and forth. I have caused death; I am not the savior I have thought. I have failed.

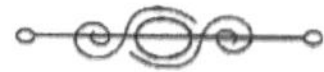

A bright flash of light blinds me, but instead of fading, it seems to grow moth-like wings that continue to spread out around us. The light is warm and calming. Then it comes closer and turns to wisps of light, random and intangible, lighting the air on fire. I think for a moment, is it my imagination. No, it is real. First there is just one, then there are several.

Clark and several others have run ahead. Broken communications lets me and my men know the Commander, our captain, has come aboard. I order the men out once more, but when we try to follow the maps on our wrist, where there were once paths there are now walls. The alien ship is twisting and bending. It is like we have been swallowed by some infernal creature that is now diving and turning its body, opening and closing parts of itself, fighting us like we are some kind of disease.

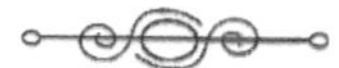

Clark! In the confusion, the emotion, the link, I have forgotten the most important thing. My link will be the strongest now, his mind almost mine as I delve into it. No matter the pain, my thoughts splintering as I enter. Their primitive minds are not meant for this, my mind is not. But I must fix what I have started. Clark, please Clark, let me make this right!

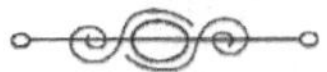

The corridors pass by quickly as my legs turn to jelly. My chest burns and my throat constricts. I swallow as I turn to look behind me, the action tearing at my dry throat. Tears welled from the pain, the liquid adding a frosted ambiance to the ships internals as that light bursts behind me again. Why? Why was it, why are they coming for me? What had I done?

Oh, yeah, I entered its body, tried to mess with its insides, change its personality, its shields, and now... now I was paying the price, just like my crew mates, my acquaintances, and anyone else that was stupid enough to come aboard. We are dead, the ship knows it, they know it, and I know it. But I am not about to give up. It would be easy to. My body is burning, chest exploding, legs pulsating, throbbing, and every part of me is hurting. My head pounds as I push myself to my final limits.

An explosive force smashes into my cheek in a flash, and my head is thrown sideways. Stumbling I cry out in pain, horror, terror. When will this be over? Something strikes my shoulder, shredding my suit and tearing my flesh. I smash into the wall, my shoulder burning. Blood oozes from me as I stumble on, grabbing for anything to keep my body upright. My legs fail me as I continue. Arching, my back caves under another blow, this time bringing me to my knees as the light circles me.

Blood is salty within my mouth, dripping from my lips; my head sways forward, my vision haloing the beautiful creature before me. Its body is luminescent in the darkness that I had become accustomed to. I cannot take my eyes from it, just as I had been awed at the vessel from the outside, now I appreciate its inhabitants from the inside. What beauty, what... gurgling, my throat is being crushed by its large hands as it grips and lifts my face to its own.

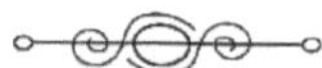

Blood in my mouth, not of my own, but a weird taste. The warmth upon my lips, head swaying with my body as I cradle myself again. My brother, my sister, my mother before me; I cannot stop the feelings within me, they flood out, my love confusing Clark as he stands in awe. Pain, throat, my mind, must stop them, my brethren. Must regain link. No time, lips taste something now, my blood on my lips. I feel my eyes roll back as I push my mind, seeking those that are close. My throat is crushed as I join,

the voices so beautiful as I hear them again. Clark, my brethren, please, please make this right!

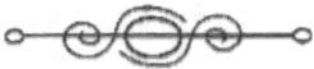

"Why?" Music, the voice is like music in my mind. "Why did you enter our sanctum?" As though an angel singing to me, it continued. "Why have you killed my brethren? Why did you take life?"

All these words swim in my head, the thoughts as though sung as its large jaws open and it bites down. Flailing, I try to stop it, my fists punching, and then there were no fists. My appendages flailing, blood splattering the ships walls, my life force spurting from me.

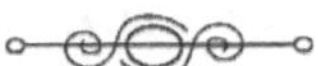

Nooooo! Stop, this one can save us, this one can communicate, be our conduit. He can be made to understand. Go no further. I lay my body between them; if they want to tear him apart, limb from limb, they must do so to me first. I am weak, my life waning as the claws tear at my mind, wanting revenge for their loss. No, we are not this, we are...

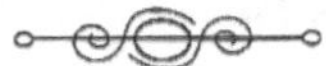

"You!" The voice is back, no more singing, but yelling, splitting my head like a hammer, intrusive to the point of agony. "You are the one."

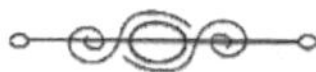

It drops me, my face planted on the floor with a thud. Its bony feet feel heavy upon my back, the clawed toes digging into my shoulder as it stands on me, keeping me pinned to the ground. I can feel its hands lower onto my head, almost massage my scalp, then its nails. One by one, it sticks them through my skin, one by agonizing one it thrust its claws into my skull, tearing through the last bits of sanity I have left... and I pass out.

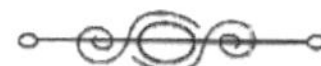

I welcome the darkness, the thoughts of my own mind, and the subtle reflection of the past events. However, the screams; they are in pain, their only hope now lost in his slumber, his body too weak to instantly accept the joining. His vessel, his mind must rest for now. Hopefully when we awake he will be one with me, with us, but until then I too sleep.

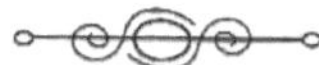

I am not sure for how long I have been dragged down the corridors, my bloodied stumps dragging upon the floor. The creature's body engages the ship as it walks, as though its power is bringing the ship to life as it passes.

The beautiful voice resonated inside my head again. "Not me. You."

Oh my head. The throbbing; the pain; the splitting agony. I raise my arms, my mind telling my hands to grasp my head, to massage the pain away. But to no avail, the pain not quelled by the touch of my throbbing stumps.

"Soon," said the voice again. "Soon, we can go home." Beauty, the creature before me, looking into my eyes, it's loving, caring, angelic, eyes. "Soon we go home and leave these demons." The voice petered off. "This hell."

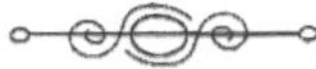

Some small hope through the pain that now rapes my body. He is listening, hearing our song; I relax my thoughts, and allow the others to enter, not wanting to overload his feeble mind. But I stray too far; the emotions of the other drag me to him, this one that calls himself Bines.

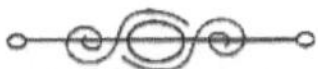

Clark is lost. The Commander is lost. I alone found my way to some kind of monitoring station. I must have killed a dozen or more creatures on my way down. Giant mirrors now surround me, reflecting and projecting images of myself and the crew of both ships. I watch helplessly as my crewmates fall, their weapons not doing a damn thing. A creature carries Clark through maze after maze. Occasionally it seems to stare up at me, and straight into my soul. Every time I have that feeling of déjà vu, again and again, as if I had been here before, as if I have watched this before.

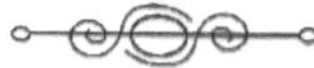

No, this is not what I wanted; he was supposed to be a savior. Why is he killing, why are we killing, this is too much. The anger; the pain; the death... we need to seal them in, stop the pain, the carnage, the infliction that is humanity.

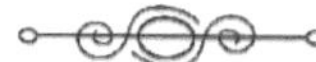

I have no have time to react. The glass seems to encase me, surround me. It is like a cocoon. I feel like I can't breathe. I watch my fellow soldiers break through wall after wall and I watch the Commander scream, "Kill the beast!" I watch helplessly as they do their worst to destroy the alien vessel and anything not human. Creatures come and go from the shadows devouring and dissolving the only family I have, and there is nothing I can do. It is as if I have become caught up inside of a nightmare. My body is frozen.

In a moment I am standing above a corridor. Blood burns inside my veins, swelling them, raising them inches above the bones in my hands. It is unlike anything I have ever felt before. Then, just as the pain becomes too much to bear and I feel as though I will burst, there is nothing, not even fear. I stand, out-of-body, staring down at a creature between my own men and Clark. I still have my rifle, so I point it at the demon.

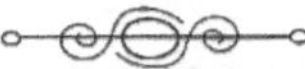

We have become one, inflicted ourselves upon each other's minds. The intersection of our bodies has pushed our bond, made it strong. Now we see as I see from above, joined, the three. No, not this way, no Bines, do not shoot! Clark, run, run, run!

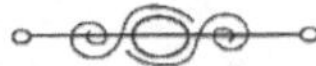

It throws its body between us, the military men and me. It stops the cascade of weapons fire, now ripping at its flesh, stopping the surely fatal collision of the projectiles and my own frail shell. And then they are upon them. The men scream, yelling for their lives, and praying for their deaths. The angels swoop down. Their large jaws, razor claws, ripping through armor, weapons, and souls as they damn us to hell for our blasphemy.

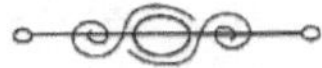

Pain. The wounds. The projectiles have torn me, ripped apart my flesh, and my life is waning. So many voices, so much pain, the screaming, the loss. I must break this cycle; I must... must help Clark to understand what has happened, what is happening. We must get him to the

communications, must stop this as we plead to him. Sing to his soul.

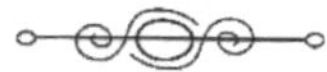

The creature that had saved me looks up at me, in its eyes I see the same love that it had shown moments earlier. Its large clawed hands trying to stop the luminescent fluid from spurting from its wounds. It knows that it is over, that its life is forfeit. But it holds my focus, its angelic voice singing to me as black tears drip down its scaly face.

"You, our savior. Take my people home. Please. Take my children home." It talks to me, but it doesn't open its mouth as its eyes glaze and they lose focus, its hand outstretched as a door opened before me. *Are we that close? Has he died only a meter from his goal? What do I need to do?* These things fill my thoughts, as that angelic song fills my mind. "We are the children, the children of the one. We come in peace, we come as one. We love all that is alive, true and sublime. Please help my children. Please help them survive."

In my mind, an angelic form walks the corridors, its children playing around it as they make their way to the airlock. It reaches out as it nears the men, reaching out to the Commander. It does not perceive his raised rifle as a threat, the knife at its end a deadly weapon. But before the angel's hand touches the Commander's head, his rifle's blade pierces its chest; its eyes glaze but are not lifeless.

The ship reacts dramatically, a time loop being generated, the parties from each ship, human and alien made to re-enact this incident again and again, a steady distress beacon emanating from this gigantic being, until now...

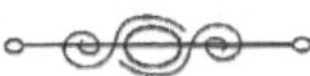

He knows what started this, now we must... we must tell him of, of our customs, of our love for life. My children, so do I miss them, our mother, my mother, my father... my mind wanders, I hope with all my heart my brethren can stop this as I fear I will last little more, my mind is fading.

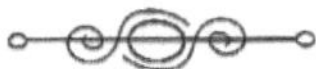

The image is simultaneous to another, but not from that time. Many years have passed. My mind filled with the first moment that we had entered the ship, those few seconds that it took me to access controls, re-route systems before the creature startles us, its claws stretching out and trying to rip our heads from our bodies, then the gunfire. The military guns tearing through the creature. It turns, its claws lashing out, Frigit's throat torn open.

The images haze together, forming another. Two of the creatures stand, their arms outstretched as they come closer. Their hands cupping each other's skulls as though trying to shake them loose. Feelings of warmth wash over me, the vision of beauty as wisps surround them. They let go; their eyes alight in love as they step away. The wisps joined, dancing between them, as a movie plays for them, their most sacred memories; a child's birth; a wife's joy, a first kiss, each one sharing and appreciating the other.

They were trying to communicate with us, I thought to myself, *they were trying to show us that they meant no harm. We have killed them, hunted them and finally them us. We are the monsters, not them. We are the intruders, not them. We are the murderers, not them.*

The light follows me as I crawl, my elbows dragging me as I scrape along the uneven floor until I slump in a pile. I can hear the second team of military men mustering their rifles, yelling to their allies, demanding justice. *I cannot let this happen again. I cannot let them kill more innocents.* Further I struggle, my failing body screaming at me to give up. My mind is black with the numbing pain that wracked my entire body. Footsteps, running, faster, louder, screams, gunfire...

The door closes, and there is silence.

The little dragon stares at me. Its large eyes and weird snout turned sideways enquiring to my presence. "You are not Pilot," it sung inside my head, "You are wrong, you killed my children."

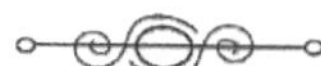

I must intervene. I can feel the regret, the loss, the need for vengeance. I can sense the doubt as our overseer

greets Clark with hostile words. "I... He must be pilot, we have no other. He will communicate with them, show them we mean no harm, share our love. Only he can make them see. Pilot he must be." Clark's own thoughts, words, they drown out my own as he pleads.

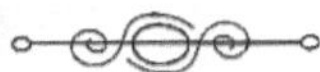

"I did not know. W... we thought you were attacking us... that you were trying to..." my thoughts flood out of me, my feelings of regret, of sorrow, of the horror I have faced and the suffering of both sides.

"Thank you, you are Pilot. Must be Pilot. Pilot is our shepherd; he protects us. We welcome you. Will you take us home?" The creature sang into my mind as my thoughts were filled with beauty, a planet self contained, with no war, only love.

"How?"

"With your mind Pilot, with our mind. With your body, with our body."

The home planet becomes clear, the path to take, and the years of travel. It is all clear to me, to them. There is a chair here, the Pilot's chair; I pull myself up, struggling to stay conscious, and collapse into it. My stumpy arms tingle, light emanating from them. Parts of the ship climb along the arm of the chair, vines entering my arms. I scream and blackness followed.

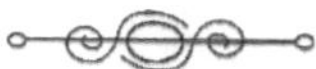

He is one with us, this Clark; I see the beauty, the love, but also the pain and loss. We were not meant to encounter these humans, not meant to make contact. They are too young, too selfish, and too instinctive. They need time, and if they survive, then and only then should we join with them! Please, if you are listening to this, if you pick up this transmission, please heed my words, but do not blame them, as it is their nature as love is ours.

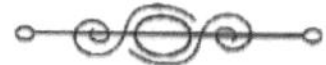

I need no hands to feel, no eyes to see, I can see clearly, the world around me opens. Space, life, the delicate balance between it, it was clear to me in this moment, in the completion of the joining of the ship and I. My thoughts go back. Back to the first contact, twenty years before. The military ship and its men being sent a capsule, a peaceful offering. That capsule stayed upon their ship, being studied, poked and prodded. The capsule was alive, it screamed for mercy for twenty years before the second vessel came. Whilst the men, the military men and this ship were captured in a time vortex, their weapons rendered useless, the ships inhabitants frozen in time. It was a self-defense mechanism, not a very practical one; fight or flight. They had not encountered dangerous situations before; they had not known this would happen. Then I came. Visions of the capsule again, screaming, wanting to be one with its people; back with its parents; back with the ship. The bridge, the military vessel, the injection; It was all clear. I had been injected with the DNA from the capsule, but something was different this time to when others had been injected, someone had triggered a reaction inside of me. One that had allowed me to enter the ship freely, to change its shields, to release the stasis.

Noooooooo! It was I that had allowed this slaughter, I who had killed these children. It was I who had caused their pilot to die. I could see it all clearly now, as though it had happened in seconds, not decades. *It was all my fault.*

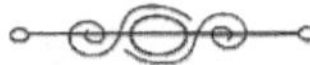

Yes Clark, we created this; I created this. My joining with you allowed your entry, our combined demise, but you can stop this, you can. My head slumped, mind going, life waning, I must see this through as I inject the poison into my body again. Not long now and it will be over but for now you must continue to see.

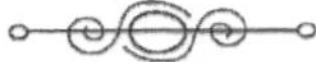

"And the others?" My mind searches the ship, finding the military men, their killing spree continuing. I can feel the pain as another of my brethren succumb to their callous machines.

"It is of your will, my Pilot. Of your will." the voice held no hint of anger, the beauty only amplified at its words. "But heed my warning. The Pilot before you befell their treachery." The image of our first contact sprang into my mind again, of the one that was angelic in appearance. This was the pilot, the one that kept his children safe and ultimately the one that had let them down by trusting us.

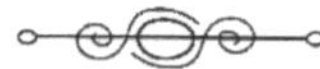

Emptiness, loneliness, loss; these are my thoughts; they are his as he draws me to him again. I need to get back, to help Clark in my minutes before my demise, but for now Bines becomes me as he enters his past and walks his now lonely ship.

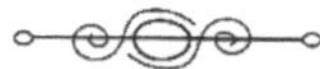

I walked through an empty ship. It was nothing more than a hollow shell now. I could see in front of me a large capsule, a part of the alien object... only now it was on board the Geras! I watched like a shadow as I, and even the Commander, experimented on the capsule. What had we done? How long have we been playing this game, repeating the same events of betrayal over and over before putting ourselves into the deep sleep? I have forgotten so much.

This time though things were different. The second ship had added a new variable to our game of murder, rinse repeat. The symbols on the wall around me appear clearly now. My mission isn't one of first contact or discovery; my mission is salvage by any means necessary.

They never should have trusted us.

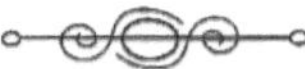

Clark's emotions ripped me from the remorse of Bines, maybe there was hope, but not now. They are too SAVAGE. Noooo! Whyyyyyyy?!

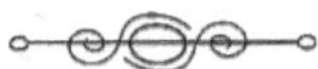

No, I have spared their lives, why are they doing this? Why do they feel that we own this ship and the beautiful creatures upon it? Our shields are holding, but they are not going to last. I modified them when I came aboard, and now they are using my modifications against me. "Why, why, why? I don't want to kill you!" I scream.

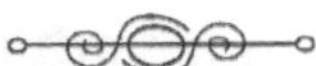

Waning... my mind, body, only seconds now. I will not see this end; will not be privy to its course, yet Bines beckons me one last time.

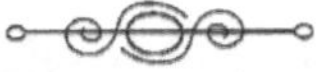

Rinse. Kill. Repeat. For twenty years we fought and we are trapped.

I feel my soul return to my body inside the Geras.

I no longer have a reason to remember.

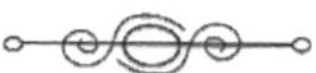

As our journey comes to an end, our vessel upon theirs, my last breath escapes me, and upon it I call our savior's name, Clark...

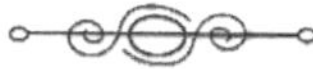

"Why, why, why? I don't want to kill you!" I scream again. This time there is a reply:

"Because they can. They are a poison, they must be eradicated." The voice sounds like the ones I am connected to, but it is different. It does not sing; it is bitter, wrong, and aggressive. A dark ship, like the one I am upon, appears before me. The ship was another; it had just arrived in the fray. The dark voice continues; "We have been coming for you, we have been twenty years to your rescue." It has none of the beauty that I was mesmerized with when I first saw the ship I am upon and to which I am now connected. It is as though diseased by years of suffering, years of hearing its children cry out in pain, years of living for one thing, a death bringer. "We have seen all that has befallen you. We will save you. We will free our children, our wives, and our husbands. Now we will end this. We will end them. There is no place for them here. And then we will return home, raise an army and we will eradicate them from our space and then theirs." The dark ship is turning to our ships, the humans, and its intent is obvious.

The little dragon appears before me again as the black ship opens fire, the military vessel changing it's targeting from us to counter the new threat. The dragon's eyes bare blood as it cries, the beauty in its voice filled with sorrow. "We cannot let this get home. We cannot let this disease of anger reach our children, our wives, and our husbands. We cannot let this happen." I understand what is required, what is asked of me. I ask if they know what is asked of them. They respond, singing to me in unison, singing the song of their people as they close their eyes one last time and I obliterate all of those from around us.

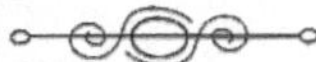

Concept idea given to authors to write story = A crew aboard a salvage ship, encounters a ship drifting through space. As they attempt to enter, they discover that only organic material can pass through a force field protecting the ship from intruders. With the unmanned drifter floating away from them, the crew tries to work out a way to cover the growing distance without the aid of modern technology.

D.C. Daines resides in Western Australia and is the author of The Star Crystal.

Stephen Landry is a 26 year old graphic designer living in Nashville,Tn. His work has been seen on TV, in magazines, and on the web. Current projects include writing a full length novel and creating illustrations and cover art for up and coming authors, video game companies, and film studios.

Blood and Dragons

BY OWEN D. GODFREY

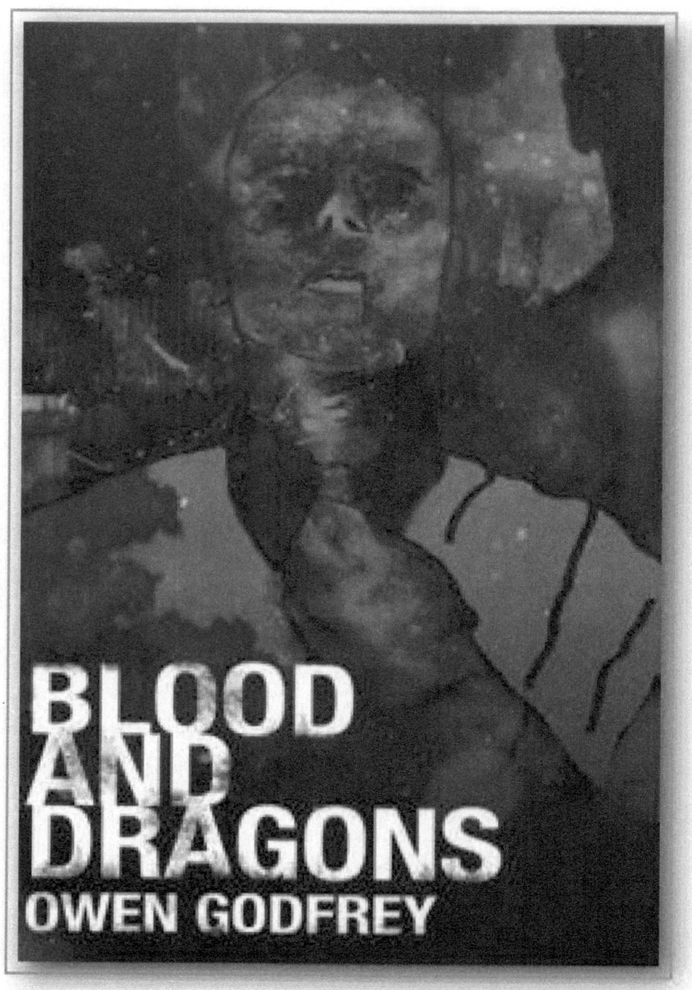

I lay awash in a pool of warm bodies and pleasant dreams, nestled against my charge as she slept, but I knew that a change had occurred. That mind, so dark and intriguing, that mind, so lost within its own twisted labyrinths; that mind had been missing, and now it was back. I knew, with a certain dark amusement, what had happened, so I settled the others, closed my eyes, and sought out that mind in the darkness…

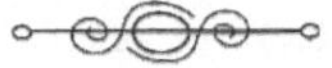

Bedon knelt; a naked supplicant to the gruesome masterpiece of the room. Blood dripped from his body, along with unidentifiable pieces of flesh. With each gasp, his lungs filled with the room's charnel stench. Sluggishly, his mind sought coherence. '*I must,*' he thought, *'have penetrated her bowel.*' He looked around sharply, suddenly alarmed that there might have been a witness, and for an instant his mind slipped… *his father kneeling across from him over his mother's body, holding the bloody knife. His face… horrified, appalled, begging his son for… something…*

He banished the image with a slash of his beautiful knife, sending a trail of blood spots across the pretty pink duvet on the bed. He focused on the blade, watching the gas-light glitter off the silvery edge, following the dripping blood down to where the fat drops hung, glowing slightly with the fading thaumatic energy from the woman's body… from there to the loose line of blood drops on the duvet. '*Follow the trail, and join the dots, until you find the…*' His eyes fell to the floor. '*Is that a piece of liver or kidney?*'

Fatigue and fugue pulled at his mind as he stood. He counted his heart down to a steady pace… 10, 9, 8, 7… until he could start to recall details.

He hadn't intended to kill the woman — "the whore" as he thought of her — not yet anyway. This was supposed to have been just a pleasure visit; scouting for his real visit on Alva's Eve. It was a mess, but… nothing had changed, it was just sooner than he'd intended.

He lifted his head, fatigued muscles screaming. Focus… where, when… and something. It was dark out, and he could see the lights of the outskirts; southern edge of the city, the cheap part of town. '*Yes,*' he thought. '*Hotel… the Arcadia… traveling prostitute… a traveling prostitute with Alusian blood… I remember. She must have had an ancestor from Tharlia at least two generations back, no more than three.*'

There were twelve sapient races of Xanadu, or at least there were twelve acknowledged by the Tahlicy as creations of the Gods, and therefore accorded all the rights of civilization. The four dominant races were the Aluse, the Valan, the Humans and the Ren. The Aluse of Tharlia dominated the world with thaumatics, followed closely by the Valan of Varland, now Slasiland after Tharlia took it over in the war. The Humans and the Ren were the two dominant non-thaumatic races.

He looked around the squalid hotel room. He spied his clothes in the bathroom, mercifully free of any stains. He checked the window, carefully avoiding making himself visible from below. '*Third floor, looking out to the Southeast. Lamps are all still lit, so lots of time before dawn. I can easily get home and some shut-eye before tomorrow. Then,*' he thought contemptuously, '*I will let my daytime self wake up, and waste such a wonderful day sitting at a desk.*'

He was beatific now, with the calm that came after a kill. His well-tuned body was recovering quickly from the exertion; his liver and kidneys filter and processing his blood, bringing him back to normal. '*I suppose,*' he thought idly as he prodded a piece of the woman's own liver or kidney with his toe, '*that I should be more concerned with my circumstances.*' There was time, but dawn would eventually come. It was winter, so the suns always rose an hour or so early, especially Gransel's Sun. However that Sun would be dim and cool before Lydel's Sun took over in the late morning. That would keep people indoors until they had to get up to walk to work. '*I have to get back earlier,*' he thought, '*but I only have to watch out for the night-carters and the lamplighters. So long as I stay to the edges of the city, I'll have no problems.*'

He nodded to himself and smiled; it was good to have a plan.

He puzzled over some of the pieces of flesh around him. There seemed to be too many pieces really, but he supposed it was about right. He wasn't sure why he lost control, after all, he believed he was never angry, that he never lost control or was ever afraid. Most of all, he was certain that he was never afraid, and he never, EVER, lost control. He was sure he couldn't have lost control… so he must've been in control. '*Yes,*' he thought, '*I must have always have intended it to happen this way… I planned this, I just… didn't know it.*'

He realized suddenly that she still had her eyes, so he quickly removed them. For him the eyes were the most important thing; not just a signature, but also a trophy that he could *absolutely* not do without.

He caught sight of himself in the hotel's dresser mirror. He was a handsome man with a good body that now was liberally splattered with gore. That body had been keenly trained in the services, but was softer now, although he still enjoyed the effect of looking at himself, especially this way. He looked for the scars from the war once more, but there were none; they'd been careful to remove all evidence of what they'd done once they found out who he was. He considered himself beautiful, and he was both proud and resentful of the work the Tharlian's had done.

'My daytime self should look at himself more often,' he thought, *'and appreciate what a work of art we are.'* He smiled to himself and held out the grisly trophies in his hand; enjoying the idea of the horror his daytime self would feel if he could see this image. He even tried to wake him up a little, but of course he couldn't. He laughed. He also felt slightly agitated, but quietly quashed that feeling because he never felt agitated.

He quickly showered and dressed, carefully avoiding any more of the blood and viscera. He inspected the room with a critical eye for evidence. For a sloppy evening, it was all fairly good. He checked himself in the mirror and smiled. A handsome man, yes, but once he put on a nice gentleman's suit, he was something else. He wore a nice madrona vest with a silk puff tie over a classic high club-collared shirt and a nice tweed frock coat. Over that he wore a wartime great coat against the cold, a souvenir that he'd kept from the war, and last of all a nondescript bowler. The last two afforded him some anonymity as opposed to being fashionable. *'Ah,'* he thought, *'if my daytime self could see me now!'* He looked around at the mess and chuckled.

He remembered how he grew up as he straightened his tie. Under his mother's abuse and love, and his father's thumb, as it wouldn't do for bruises to be seen. The son of the High Tahl — the theoretical religious leader of

Xanadu but also the Head of State of Basland Theocracy — was always very carefully dressed in public. He remembered… the despair in his father's eyes when he spotted a new bruise or scratch, and the fights that came after. His mother's loving embrace, and her anger and disgust that he hadn't inherited any of her Alusian "magic" — her thaumatic graces — just the eyes, the eyes she loves so much, that can see thaumatic fields. The pain as his mother hits him — he is 5 — then hits him again and again, till he can see nothing, just smell the blood and alcohol, and feel the pain. Then it stops, and suddenly he is 13, and he opens his eyes to see his father bleeding, fighting with his mother who is holding a knife. That such a tiny woman can wield such force… Bedon gets up, holds her and pulls her off him, and together he and his father push her down and hold her as she screams. His father wrestles the knife from her hand, and she screeches something Bedon doesn't understand… but the knife comes down… and then… that shocked, horrified look on the High Tahl's face, as he looks at his son, his accomplice.

He shook himself again, surprised to see that the mirror was smashed. His hand was bleeding, apparently from smashing the mirror. He went to the sink, and there, carefully and without shaking, he washed the knife and collected the eyes from where he'd left them. He carefully wrapped up his injured hand, and then searched his pockets for one of the little evidence bags that he always carried with him. His flashbacks were particularly severe, leaving him worried that he might make some trivial but costly mistake… although, of course, he *never* worried. However, the thrill of what he did was all about the exhilaration he'd felt back then when his mother… and so the flashbacks were in some ways the best part. Also the feeling of finally sharing something special with his father… not to mention the power and freedom he'd felt. Definitely, never to mention those.

His "special" eyes helped him recognize the taint of thaumatic blood in what he saw as "half-breed whores". They could hide it from everybody else, most didn't even know themselves, but his eyes could tell.

He looked around one last time and opened the door to leave. A man was standing there, looking surprised. *'The pimp? I hadn't thought to check.'* The man smiled amiably, then looked past Bedon into the room and looked confused. He looked even more confused as he noticed the knife sticking out of his belly... but Bedon put a hand over his mouth and pushed up with his knife so the man couldn't scream. That was a tactical error though; as the man stepped back he tumbled over the balcony. Bedon looked over the edge to see him crash squarely into the back of a night cart. The horse panicked at the shock, and bolted, leaving the Pargan cart-man standing there, confused and holding a bucket of piss and shit in his hands. Bedon pulled back before he looked up, and waited. The night-carter was yelling angrily and chasing after his horse and cart, but clearly he hadn't understood just what had landed in the back. Bedon smiled. '*Well, how auspicious,*' Bedon thought, '*remove the filth and remove the evidence.*' He returned to the room to quickly clean the blood from his hand and knife, and then headed for the stairs.

There was nobody else on the next landing, just a small dragon toasting a rat. Of the night carter there was no evidence. The dragon hissed at him, and that distinctive shiver of scales traversed its body from snout to tail; it could smell the trace of blood, and it was spooked by smell. It grabbed its rat, jumped up onto the railing and launched itself off the balcony.

Small dragons are truly appalling fliers; we're the only dragon species able to survive and thrive in a low thaumatic environment, but we were also the only species that was likely to break its neck in a fall. This one was better than most, it headed towards the next balcony one floor below and barely managed to avoid killing itself on a brick wall. It lost its rat though, and two other small dragons took advantage. Bedon watched all this with wry amusement.

He shook his head, exasperated with himself. *'I'm watching dragons for Gransal's sake!'* He ran down the stairs, but stopped himself and started to walk slowly. *'The boys in blue will be here in… 45 minutes tops,'* he thought. *'No point in running, people notice people running.'*

He left the building by the Southern stairwell, heading away from the valley, then turned to the East to skirt around the edge of the escarpment. Thousands of kilometers away to the South, on the edge of the world, he could see the spire of Samusa's God Tower against the sky. At least 700 km tall and invisible in the night sky to all eyes, except to those like his. To his eyes, it swirled with its distinctive energies. *'Oh,'* he thought, *'what stories must unfold behind the backdrops of this world!'*

The city wasn't large; he could probably walk across it in two hours. His apartment was closer than that though, but he decided to go home via the park so there would be less chance of being seen… plus the park had a waterfall with a wonderful view of the lowlands all the way to New Bronton. The only risk was of being spotted by a lamplighter, but it was too early for them, and he was uncertain if the park was even lit on a Lydel's night. Last night, yes, for the weekend, but this morning everybody was supposed to be at work, and since the council was busy cutting back again, probably they wouldn't bother lighting the park.

He kept to the back lanes when he could. A truck passed by, but mostly all he saw was the usual dray and cab, as it was too cold for people to be out on foot. There were small dragons everywhere it seemed, hunting, fighting for territory, fighting for food, mating, chasing dogs... sometimes it seems like they were trying to do all those things at once. Most were fat house pets that couldn't fly an inch, but the fat ones had more steam in their breath, so were more likely to win a fight. They could broil a rat in less than a minute.

He saw a drunken woman sleeping it off in a lane behind a pub, but he resisted the urge to check her eyes. Within ten minutes, he'd arrived at the park and it was as dark as he'd hoped.

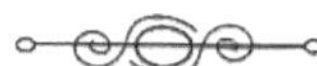

I sighed and stood up, shrugging my way out of the pile. It was beginning to look like Bedon was going to make himself a problem for me. I really hated interfering, and his mind was fun to watch, but... I had my responsibilities. I shook myself, stretched and climbed up onto the rock. Maybe I'd be lucky and he'd just miss noticing her altogether.

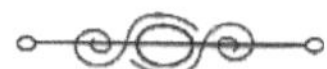

To Bedon, the park was beautiful at night. There was little to see, but the valley ended here in a waterfall that roared over the edge of the escarpment. It wasn't a huge waterfall, the river was barely more than a creek here, but with all the rain they'd had lately, it had become spectacular. In the distance he could just see the lights of New Bronton, slightly more than a hundred kilometers away. *'I wonder what father is doing tonight?'* Some Tharlian plants, drelias mostly, had been planted here, and although they didn't have the thaumatic field strength they really needed to thrive well here, they still grew and to Bedon's eyes they made the park glow with life in the darkness. *'I really must come back here some evening,'* Bedon thought. *'I'll pack a midnight snack and blanket and just enjoy it.'*

He noticed something moved to his right, near the waterfall. He stopped and discretely moved deeper into the shadows, and watched as his eyes adjusted to the low light. The drelias were a distraction now; glowing slightly, and moving gently in the breeze coming down the valley, they made it hard to see anything else. He jumped as the shadow at his feet moved and hissed at him. It was a small dragon, glowing only slightly with its own thaumatic light. He rolled his eyes and hissed back at it, and then kicked it away, but it came back growling. We are thaumatic creatures really, so he could see it faintly in the dark once his eyes had adjusted, but the drelias were still brighter. In Tharlia, where his mother came from, the thaumatic field was very strong and some of our species that grew to 30 meters in length, and breathed real fire, but in Basland, we were smaller than the average dog… although most dogs had the sense to avoid us.

He could see a rock ledge over where he had first seen it. There were more of us he saw. About eight or ten, all crowded under the ledge. We were curled up around a small figure covered in a duvet of all things, and his eyes knew the thaumatic lines of that figure. *'Haiku Sir-Tor! What on Xanadu is she doing here?'* he thought. *'She should be at home with her wife. Did they fight?'*

He didn't know the answers and he really didn't care. He felt his daytime self rise. That self had a crush on that tiny half-Valan lady, and would want to protect her and take her home. He squashed that self down. *She's mine now, not yours,* he thought. He smiled and pulled out his knife. He'd never dared hoped for an opportunity like this. Normally, he couldn't touch her, because she worked the same place as his daytime self, and it would be too suspicious if she were killed in the way he wanted to. Here and like this though… priceless. He could almost believe in the gods for this opportunity.

The woman was a half Valan, half Human, and just as his mother's people — the Aluse — were able to manipulate thematic energy, the Valan could do so too, although not directly. Instead they crafted thaumatic technologies, and had a reputation as engineers. Haiku certain did; Bedon knew for certain that she might be one of her people's greatest engineers. Both were a small race though, although Valan were naturally much taller. Haiku herself was barely the size of a young teenager, although she would have been counted as a giant among full bloods. She worked as an engineer at the school, doing research and building things that Bedon secretly detested. But he liked her still… '*No,*' he thought angrily, *'my daytime self likes her, I detest her and all she stands for! Basland is for Humans!'*

He edged over to the rock ledge, and smiling, he reached for the duvet.

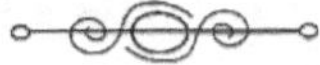

I sighed and stood up. I cleared my throat to get his attention, but for some reason the idiot just refused to notice me standing there on the rock in front of him.

That's when the small dragon bit him.

It latched onto his forearm hard, biting through overcoat, jacket, shirt and flesh, almost to the bone, and it started cooking the wound. Bedon swore, then grabbed it and swung it against the rock ledge, right next to me, giving me the second fright of the night. I heard the poor things bones break, and as Bedon felt them, he reveled in the sensation. Then he took his knife and cut the small dragon open, and flung the carcass down on the rock beside me.

Here was a most disturbing thing; not the killing, and not the death of one I had counted as a friend, but rather it was that I had watch him through the mind of his killer, and watch him die through his own mind too. I had known him, that dragon; a fellow of infinite jest, of most excellent fancy; he bored me to tears a thousand times; and now, what a mess! Well, never mind; the world has many small dragons.

Worst of all, Bedon STILL hadn't noticed me there.

He pulled up his sleeves and examined his arm. The dragon's teeth were small, but his arm was badly gashed. The steam burn was mild so far as he could tell, but he needed to get to some proper light. He wrapped it up in a handkerchief. Through all that, the girl — my charge — had barely moved, and the other dragons were simply made more restless. *'Girl?'* he thought, *'She is close to a century older than me, however she appears.'* He wondered about the lack of reaction; the killing had not been at all quiet.

I sighed and shook my head.

As he reached for her again I stopped him: "That's enough Bedon," I said, "this one isn't for you."

He looked up. Another small dragon — myself — sat upon the ledge, and he almost looked away, looking for the source of my voice... but then he noticed my eyes. Ordinary dragon eyes on the surface, but to his eyes they were now a vortex of thaumatic energy. He glanced from my eyes to the tower in the distance and back again, identifying the same pattern of energy within. '*A god avatar,*' he thought, '*but which one?*'

Superficially calm, a very nasty shock ran through his body that he refused to acknowledge. For all the experiences he had had in his lifetime, he'd never really believed in the gods, and seeing the utter humanity of his father — who tradition taught should be the avatar of a god — so graphically displayed, had utterly convinced him that we didn't exist. '*It's not Hymathra,*' he thought, '*or I'd be dead or arrested for murder now.*'

I rolled my eyes; '*as if she'd care,*' I thought to myself.

'*It's not Santali,*' he continued thinking, '*or the mad goddess would have just slaughtered me.*' that caused me a serious chuckle; he hadn't taken a good look inside himself for a long time.

'*Samusa wouldn't approve,*' he thought, '*and Gransal wouldn't care unless there's a war on somewhere or unless there's a game to be played, otherwise he'd have dealt with me long ago. As for Lydel... he just wouldn't be here. But there's only one that traditionally uses dragons as his avatars...*'

"Alva," he said out loud.

I smiled. "Don't you have to be somewhere Bedon Wals? Such as... home to bind your wounds, home to avoid your own father's forces? Home hiding from your daytime self?"

He glared at me, and then defiantly wiped his blade on my neck. That little act of defiance certainly ticked me off, but not enough to make me make him stop. I never really appreciated what a loathsome piece of work he was until I had him up close. I smiled at him, and licked the blood off. It was my nicest smile, well, from me it was anyway. "You'd best run."

Bedon wanted to kill me… we avatars are mortal after all; we can be killed… theoretically. And damn he wanted to cut out my eyes for his collection. However… his daytime self was there in the background, still asleep, but reacting with fear and awe even so. His night-time self didn't know what fear was. I mean literally; when the Tharlians had tinkered with his noggin, they thought it would be best to make him think he was fearless, so he had no idea what personal fear was. He was anger, he was retribution, and he was the Gods' Damned Collector. All that was on the surface though, and everything else about him was an insufferable ass. But that phase surfaced in his mind.

"'Gods' Damned Collector'," I said, "Very fitting. I like that. Is that what you want to be, the Gods' Damned Collector? I can arrange it."

That was the moment he peed himself. His surface mind might have no idea what fear was, but his deeper mind and body certainly did.

Bedon snarled and smiled his evilest smile at me, and raised his knife. It was shaking badly. I smiled back. Bedon looked deeply into my eyes and discovered something important; a dragon's smile much more intimidating than a human's, or even a half-human; it's the teeth really.

"You really can't back down, can you?" I asked him. "When the Tharlians captured you during the war, they split open your personality like boar eating a watermelon, and they spit out your identity like seeds. They also installed a series of commands in places where even you can't see them, one of them being to kill off anybody who is a risk of randomly exposing you. They also installed a safety phrase: 'Aloc thar'kra secra Alume'? Did I say that right? Well then, let's make this easy for all of us. Run home Bedon Wals, run home. Run as though your life depends on it. Run as though... let's see... as though the sun were rising. Don't stop running until you are inside your home with the doors locked, and then forget about this. Forget it all!"

Bedon felt me in his mind, and his sight was filled with nothing but my eyes. It was just a little push; the words took care of most of it. He was confused. The sun wouldn't rise for hours, and yet there it was on the horizon. His daytime self, as it thought of itself, half awoke, and he saw only night, but thanks to the Tharlians, night-time Bedon was now utterly convinced it was dawn.

Bedon turned and ran. He ran through the park, then through the ever-lightening streets, and he ran through the lane behind his apartment building. He ran into walls in the dark, confused as to why he couldn't see them. He sealed himself in the apartment without encountering a single person, and then stumbled in the dark.

Dark?

He opened the window a crack. It was dark outside. *'Damn trickster,'* he thought. Then he wondered *'What trickster?'*

Bedon felt confused. He remembered everything, the "Collecting", walking to the park and seeing the woman in the alley, and all the small dragons, he remembered the park… and then… and then… and then running all the way home. He looked at his arm, surprised at the punctured and singed flesh and the ruined jacket. *'Oh, the small dragon in the park! How did I forget…'*

For a moment Bedon's mind skittered around, then he showered, dressed the wound, and went to bed.

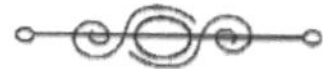

It felt like he'd slept only a few minutes when there was a pounding at the door. Groggily, Bedon sat up and went to the door. A Hymethran Officer stood there in full blues, including the short blue night-cape. "Inspector Wals… there's been another murder… it's the Collector."

Bedon stared at him. "So? I'm not in homicide, I'm security division. What do you want with me?"

"It's your father sir… the High Tahl I mean… he's ordered all available officers and divisions in Yoomba to aid finding the Collector. Sir. He did specifically name you… and your section."

Bedon ran his fingers through his hair. He was aching all over like he'd run a marathon in the night, and had no idea why. "The name of the victim?"

"Ugh… I have no idea sir. The detectives didn't care to brief me on that. Nobody important sir."

He grunted. "Well… I'd better get dressed. You have a cab for me?"

"Yes sir."

"Good. Make a pot of tea in the kitchen there, and take some out to the boys, I'll be ready shortly."

"Very good sir."

"And what's your name officer?"

"Senior Constable Breks Sir."

"Well, Constable Breks, I want you to remember, when you think about saying 'Your Father' when talking about the High Tahl, just where your career might go. It could potentially go to some very unpleasant places."

The constable removed his hat. "Understood sir."

"Now get that tea on. I'll get dressed."

Bedon got dressed quickly. He found his best clothes already laid out, but with the sleeves heavily damaged from the dragon bite. That confused him, as he had only vague memory of either wearing the suit or getting bitten. Regardless, he wrote a note for the housekeeper to get his clothes repaired and cleaned and threw the shirt in the bin. He found the trousers in the trash, soaked in urine, so he left them there, disgusted. All he could remember was a nightmare about eyes; twin eyeballs sitting in a smiling man's hand, and swirling glowing eyes over a set of very sharp teeth. He frowned and examined the jacket once more. He shook his head in disgust and headed down the stairs.

He came out to find the three officers standing on the lawn drinking tea. Along with the paddy wagon on the street, it was a sight to surely get the neighbors' chins wagging. The officers nodded to him and gave their thanks for the tea and returned their cups to the kitchen. Then they all piled into the cab, Bedon and Breks inside, the other two up top.

"Did you have a good night Sir?" Breks asked.

"No actually, I was having nightmares about the Collector."

"Ah, don't we all Sir. Being on the force, I think we see all too much of him. More than the public does."

Bedon nodded and waved his hand at the interior of the cab, which normally housed prisoners. It was an older model known as a 'Timber Trap' and should have been replaced years ago. "I thought," Bedon said, "that the Yoomba branch had been issued a motor-carriage?"

"Yes sir, but it broke down the day we used it and we don't have the budget to get it fixed… so we just keep using the cabs. I prefers them anyway sir; you always know where you stand with a horse."

Bedon nodded. "Oh and Breks, we'll be making a stop along the way. I'll have to make my section aware of what to expect… and I have a friend I have to check up on. It's important I make sure she is safe."

"Sir?"

"Breks?"

"Sorry sir… but you got the strangest confused look on your face just now."

"Did I? I had no idea. Well, you know, our job is to 'Protect All Under The Eyes of The Gods'… but some must be protected more than others… when it is the will of the gods."

"Ahhh… yes sir… I suppose that must be correct… 'By The Will of Hymathra We Serve' as they say."

"Yes."

Breks issued instructions to the driver, and they turned off towards the school, Breks staring out one window, Bedon the other. Bedon shortly spotted a small dragon sitting on the curb, watching them pass.

"Breks, has it ever occurred to you that none of us have any idea what is really going on in this world? I mean… it's like it's all just a macabre comedy for the amusement of the implacable gods, and we are just the extras, destined to live and die for their delight."

Breks watched the last of the night-carts from his own window. "Sir, I figure that Xanadu is a big world and that we're just night-carts men collecting the shit. Who really cares who really pooped it?"

Bedon laughed. I didn't. Instead, that distinctive dragon shiver traversed my body from snout to tail, but it lingered in my belly like an overcooked piece of rat. I'm an Avatar, not a God, so even I don't know the full story.

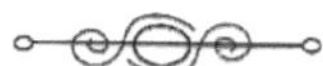

Concept idea given to authors to write story = a detective standing over a body with blood on his hands

Owen Godfrey lives in Perth, Western Australia and has been writing stories for since he was in first grade. Even class word exercises were an opportunity to make a story to bewilder the reader. Owen has mostly written for small online publications, principally Antipodean SF, and for a number of locally published fanzines. In 2010 Owen's story "Becalmed" won third prize in the Ellen Street Recovery Group Program writing competition, and was subsequently published as a part of their anthology.

Last Call

BY PAUL MASON

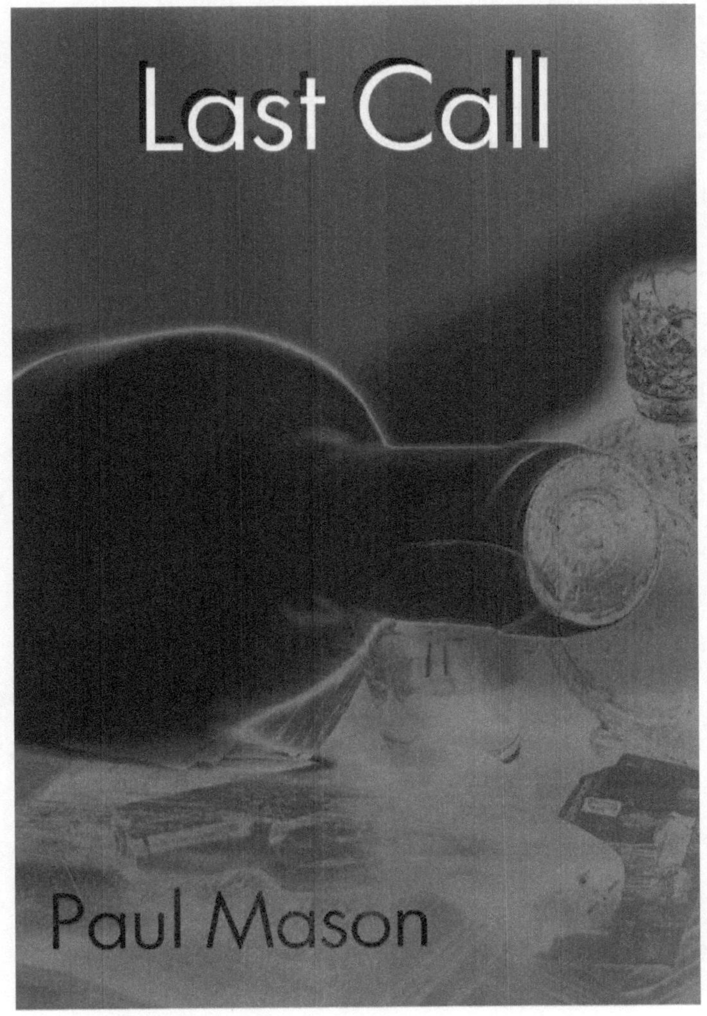

It's not often in life you get the chance to redeem yourself.

I have no dramas with admitting I've made my fair share of mistakes. Work, mates, girlfriends; you never intend to hurt anyone purposely, and we're all not blessed with the power of foresight. My loved ones: gone, left, abandoned by my actions, whatever the case; my regret was never striving to be better.

And to think, it was all from an accident, and a woman.

But I'm getting ahead of myself.

I s'pose it's tradition to start with who I am. Since I got no better place to be... or at least no choice in the matter... Oh, and let's make it clear; I might be telling you a story, but I'm not the "hero". It was never in my DNA. Had parents, but more by default than any sort of "parenting" you could point to. Mum, who I barely remember, left me and the Prick I was supposed to call "Dad" when I was little. Never found out why; never really cared. If anything, the bits I do remember were nice, but obviously, she couldn't handle the bullshit the Prick put her though.

If "Dad" — the technical name for him — was ever sober enough to respond to me, it was usually in the form of a back-hander across my mouth.

Such a way with words, my old man.

I was never good at school work; I tried when I was younger, but being small for my age meant it was a bit hard to focus, what with all the daily shakedowns and punch ups trying to keep the bullies off my back. Even with all the bullshit I put up with; I just read books when I could, and I had a knack with numbers. Probably the only thing I learnt from my old man growing up, since the races used to be the only form of noise wailing through the tinny-sounding kitchen radio.

Most kids were learning "sine", "cosine", and to find whatever the eff 'X' was. I was trying to figure out if I could score a box trifecta in Race 5 at Eagle Farm, Flemington, and Randwick.

Older blokes at the pub up the road cottoned on to this; I wasn't like the usual young kids and high school thugs they recruited for odd jobs, and "snatch 'n grabs". They probably saw me talk my way out of some scrap I got into after school one afternoon, and kept tabs on me or something. Or maybe (more likely), I was just "there" and drool wasn't hanging off the side of my mouth. Maybe one of them was a distant Uncle or something; knew my old man was barely in the picture... Who the eff knows. Point is I was given a little old-school "Numbers" running gig for a few, cheap "Lennie McPherson" wannabes.

Figured though; "running with the wrong crowd" as they say, gets you a bit of unwanted attention, and I ended up in the Nick — the one for kids. Didn't stick; just taught me to be a better crim, really. But not much better. I went bush for a while, tried to keep clean, but ended up back here, in this backward, boring town, where there were no jobs and no prospects for a down-and out, high school-dropout with my track record.

The old blokes remembered me, and vouched for me. And soon enough, I was back in the 'running' game of sorts; it was just a slight upgrade in gig that's all. Bootleg alcohol. Sure, sounds stupid, given there's no "prohibition" and all. "Dry County" type stuff. These blokes had the ability to produce liquor cheap in an old rundown distillery on the outskirts — rums, bourbon, whiskey — provide dirt cheap booze to local and interstate interests, and all unlicensed of course. But stupidly, the real gear we were trucking? Illegal cigarettes or "illicit whites" shipped in from Eastern Europe. Something to do with the plain packaging laws we have here that made it easy for them to be pushed around cheap. A couple of private shipping containers on a cargo ship, inconspicuous to almost everyone; unless you knew what you're looking for. The small dragon, painted in the bottom right corner in that black light paint shit, is the only indicator. Then, a few corrupt paperwork guys on the wharfs, and of course, the assholes I work for. Cover one illegal goods transporting with another. It never made sense to me.

So why did I get involved?

Cash.

Plus at the time, I was a "mushroom". Knew absolutely eff all... well... I "probably" could have figured it out. There were "signs": extra cargo on the trucks, stressed out dock managers, "funny" paperwork. But, I turned a blind eye for the cash. More cash than I ever saw as a "Numbers" guy. I was young and stupid; what can I say? So it was fine. For a while.

Then of course, came the accident.

I'm probably overselling it. Then again, it IS the reason I find myself here. But let me talk about her first...

It's probably the strangest situation either of us had ever been in. But after what happened, I figured that with all the stuffed up mistakes I've ever made in my own wasted life, that this opportunity to do something which will benefit my town... I had to take it.

OK, you got me. I didn't give a rat's ass about the town.

But for her...

I grew fond of that woman. Maybe too fond. Who knows? I like to think it did make me a "better" person. Who was she? Hmmn, because of what she knew and what she did, let's keep her name 'confidential'.

Helen. Let's call her 'Helen'. I like that name. Used to be a teacher in my primary school with that name I liked. She was this beautiful English woman named Helen. I was only a kid, but I knew a beautiful woman when I saw one.

But to this 'Helen'. She was English, too. Though you'd never pick it until she spoke with that soft, "Princess Diana" accent. Helen had tanned skin; an amazing tan, considering the country she came from. I'm certain that's where grey clouds are born. Or at least migrate. Anyways, She had thick, dark hair that was just a little bit longer than her shoulders. She liked to wear it up; the sporty type. Usually, a few thick strands would fall across the front of her face, either side of her cheeks as she smiled... or screamed. (Only at first though; she only screamed when we first met. Who could blame her? How ironic that I fell for this woman in the state I was in...).

She had just moved into town. I remember there were still remnants of boxes and scattered furniture around her little unit. In the mornings, the sun would shine through the kitchen window, sending light reflections bouncing off the glass tops, surfaces and other bottles congregated along the white shelves next to me. Helen was a drinker. She hadn't always been. But she was by the time I met her. She was a journalist, who had moved into the town to do her cousin a favor. She was originally a reporter from interstate, and cutbacks at the paper she was working for forced her to find something quick before her money ran out. Luckily, or unluckily, whatever your perspective might be, her cousin owned the local paper out here, and he, the bright spark, had it in his head that he, with his crack "big city reporter" cousin now available, would investigate the shonky truck movements out of town at night, like it was some sort of 'A Current Affair' special or some shit. It was a good idea, a noble idea.

Well, you can guess how it turned out.

...No. He's not dead. This isn't 'The Sopranos', idiot.

When the distillery bosses caught wind of it all, the intended investigation, they did what they did to everyone else involved.

They paid him off.

Ironically, before anyone had learnt anything. But the cousin didn't care. There was more cash in one suitcase he'd ever seen. So, the cousin pulled the story idea and "Helen" was told to let it go, and got bounced to Classifieds. Consequently, she hit the drink. That's when I met her.

She was shocked at first, didn't quite know what to say. Actually, I already mentioned it earlier; she kind of flipped out. Seriously. Screaming, carrying on. Blamed the alcohol to the point that she was pouring it into the kitchen sink. I gave her a day to calm down and sober up before I spoke to her again. I'm surprised she didn't just throw me out, but perhaps she knew something I didn't. She thought she was losing her mind. I was actually pretty excited to tell you the truth. She was the first person I'd met who could hear me. The first person I had spoken to since the accident. I had figured out her problems from being in the house for over a week, and I realized that they had tied into the corruption and bullshit from my former employer. I, as the proverbial "fly on the wall" after the accident, eventually learnt all the ins and outs of the entire distillery operation. Sure, booze and cigarettes don't hurt anyone, except maybe the folks who indulge. But the distillery was hurting people, hurting Helen. It was one of many pieces of the pie these corrupt bastards owned, and I decided if anybody could expose it, it was Helen. If she listened. Eventually, she did.

She did all the leg work, of course. I merely pointed her in the right direction. Unbeknownst to her paid-off cousin of course. It wasn't like Hollywood. There was no "wire taps", no car chases, no shoot outs, "Deep Throats", no bodies washing up on shore, nothing like that. It actually ended quite clean and boring, sorry to say for you and your interest levels. Helen took her findings to the authorities; I think the Federal police got involved and shut the whole thing down. And Helen? She landed a pretty cushy journalist gig somewhere. And I was left behind. That's OK...

Look, I told you there was no "John Wayne" moment; if anything, it was a moment of clarity for me. My life had been messed up through my own doing in a way that was irreversible. I learnt that I made stupid mistakes. So, I saw an opportunity to help a woman out of a spiraling, dark situation. I was never going to be a leading man in this. How could I be?

Now, the fact that she could hear me, well, that I can't explain. I was never a religious man, and I don't think she was, either. Heaven, Hell, who knows if either place exists or if I'm supposed to be there.

Oh, right, the accident; I keep bringing it up. I guess I should apologize too. The amount of times I mentioned it, you'd expect it to be an epic story. It really isn't. In fact, it was the stupidest thing I've ever done. I was loading alcohol into the back of one of the trucks one night, and that dodgy old distillery at night time can be hard to navigate. One of the packing guys called in sick; I had to go down into the cellar to move some things, and ended up not only locking myself down there, but a whole bunch of those rum and whiskey barrels came crashing down when I moved the wrong thing. I was there a few hours before anyone found me. Broken skull, body mangled, and drowned in barrels of bourbon, rum and whiskey.

So, that's the stupid, boring and slightly macabre way I died.

It was covered up, of course. Wouldn't want cops or anybody poking around just for the sake of some bootleg runner with no next of kin, would they? So, I "vanished". Cast aside.

But not quite. For some reason, I "lingered". I was stuck. I have no idea why. I just was. I saw and heard a lot in that distillery. A lot of private conversations occurred in the dark rooms, too. And there I was, God's sick joke, probably. Or Karma's. Who knows? Point is I was trapped. A prisoner of one of the bottles I shipped and bootlegged. Part of the significant local supply that simply got distributed to the bottlos in town. Now, I don't believe in irony, so why did I end up being picked up by the woman best placed to hear my story, and to have the right sort of reaction to it? That's not luck, any more than a dead man's essence hanging around after his time is, that's something that needed to happen, like the sun needs to come up every day. Don't need to know how it happens to say that it inevitably happens. Whatever reason; I became the property of a beautiful English woman with thick dark hair and a soft, Princess Diana accent.

And, of course, you know the rest: "Casper, the not-so-friendly ghost" stuck in a bottle of rum, with the hysterical, English, alcoholic, former journalist-slash-"Ghost Whisperer", who brought down a dodgy bootleg operation.

Talking to me snapped her out of it; she went on to get her life back. But then I had to be gotten rid of.

And now I sit, here, in a police evidence locker, where I've been for a looooong time. Boring, at times, but the company tends to have had colorful backgrounds, like me...

Who knows if Helen, or whatever her name was, still attempts to talk to bottles of alcohol on her shelf. "Hello, Bourbon?" "You got something to say to me, Whiskey?"

After all, it's not every day you learn you can talk to spirits...

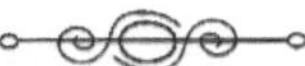

Paul Mason is a Brisbane-based writer/illustrator on 'The Soldier Legacy'; an Australian action-adventure comic series published by Black House Comics. The character and story was used as part of a national TV commercial campaign by Youi Insurance in late 2011-early 2012. He has also been published nationally and overseas, in titles such as 'The Dark Detective: Sherlock Holmes', 'Who is Killing the Great Capes of Heropa', and 'The New Adventures of the Human Fly', based on the Marvel Comics character, and real life stuntman from the 1970's. When he's not working on the next comic project, finalizing his Doctorate of visual arts, lecturing in Sequential art and drawing at the Queensland College of Art, or keeping the bills at bay, he's fighting other countries and assistant coaching for Australia in World-level ITF Taekwon-do competitions.

Age: 30

Websites:

www.facebook.com/soldierlegacy

www.pm-comic.blogspot.com

Honest to God

BY MARK ISAACSON

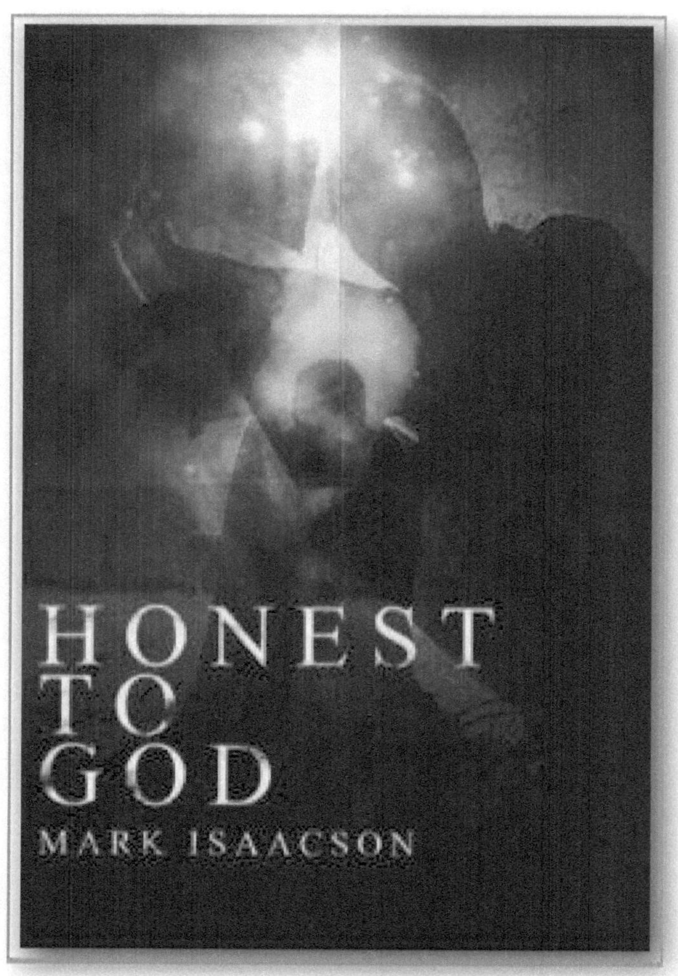

I'm no monster, but everyone is afraid of me. I've done things no-one else can do, powerful things, but instead of trying to understand what I am they've chained me up in here like an animal. It's dark, bitterness playing with my skin, but I relish it. This bleak home of mine is my one true friend, the constant companion I've longed for.

I've been due to stand trial for murder, a murder I know I committed, and they're too scared to let me out into the world again. It's been like this ever since I was born.

I was born with skin as bright a shade of white as any human eyes could bear, pupils and hair pitch black in comparison. I was no more a human than an imitation of a ghost. Doctor's dared not touch me, nurses cried at the sight of me. But my parents, they didn't see me the way anyone else did. They stood firm, held me in their arms and took me home.

Society called me unearthly. My parents called me Naomi.

The first few days were difficult at best. I wasn't a nuisance, but the rest of the family didn't appreciate me, didn't dare understand me. My Grandmother kept demanding that I be turned loose, thrown back into oblivion and forgotten about. Bless her; she wasn't really all there in that little head of hers.

My parents were overprotective in those early days, the slightest cough had them worried beyond belief. If the walls could talk, they'd tell tales of sleepless nights and endless tears, but not from me.

I was home schooled. It was both as a precaution against bullying and to ensure I was taught fairly, but I knew even then that no-one would take me. I would never be one of them, normal. But a parent's love can defy ones inability to see past their own problems, that was my first lesson.

I adored my Mother. She comforted me to no end, told me stories about mighty heroes, princesses that defied the odds. To this day I remember how warm her cuddles were, the soft fibers of her favorite jumper tickling me as I held tight.

How she managed to stay sane boggles my mind to this day. She would walk out as if nothing was wrong, dodged every verbal bullet that came her way as she worked to pay every cent it took to raise me right.

I rarely saw my Father. He worked the longest hours, kept telling Mother that he had no choice. Sometimes I would sneak out of bed to check on him and he'd chase me back. I loved that, even if it didn't happen very often, even if sometimes he was too tired to keep up. He worked so hard for us every day, but he never once complained. There was never a moment in his life that he regretted.

His heart eventually gave out when I was 15. Mother died a few years later, lung complications from all the smoking she used to do when she was a teen. I warned her that would bite her back, she knew that.

Before she died, her stories became less about fairy tales and more about the real world, the complications and challenges that humanity faced every day. We would watch documentaries instead of cartoons, learn about the world's delicate balance of mortality.

On her deathbed, Mother signed the lease of the house over to me. I was 18, just old enough to live on my own. There was no fortune waiting for me, just enough to last a few years based on flimsy insurance policies.

It took another two years before I finally crept out from behind the shadows, stood out in the open air beyond the fence that surrounded my home. I remember that day so well. The air played with my hair like a pondering child, the sun tickled my face. I ran and ran around, drawing circles in the ground with my footsteps. I only stopped once the sun went down, but then the moon took its place. No amount of fear could erase the smile from my face.

I knew then that I had to see the world with my own eyes, moving pictures just didn't do it justice. So I decided to take the next step, to go beyond my front door.

At first I disguised myself, used whatever clothing my parents left behind, a big floppy sunhat and glasses to hide behind. It worked for a time, I would scrounge around alleyways and duck behind dumpsters, befriending whatever four legged creatures dared to introduce themselves to me, until courage drew me out between other humans and crowded walkways.

I would watch them all, going about their lives oblivious to the pain and fear that surrounded them, laughing at the silliest of things or shouting at each other for no reason. Like ants, they pretend that everything they do means something, that somehow the organized chaos of their lives makes a difference to the planet they call home. So content with their lives, they fail to hear the whispers in the air.

I soaked it all in, every last drop. The longer I stayed out, the more comfortable I became, until I had convinced myself that the next step had to be taken. I wanted to talk to someone, anyone. It didn't matter who they were; a nurse, a bus driver, an old man sitting alone in a corner. It didn't matter to me. I just wanted someone to hear my voice again.

So it was, one day in September. I'd wandered into a library, trying to get out of the rain that had fallen ceaselessly since the night before. I kept to my disguise and sat opposite a young girl. She was young, pretty, with rounded black rimmed glasses and speckles on her cheeks. She was reading Anna Karenina by Leo Tolstoy.

"I've read that," I said, "it's very good."

She looked up at me, quizzically. "Oh?" she replied.

"What do you think?"

The girl paused for a moment as she put the book down. "I guess it's okay," she said finally.

"Only okay?"

The girl leaned forward, as if wanting to keep a secret. "To be honest with you, I have to read it for my literature course. I'd much prefer to read Tim Winton."

She laughed ever so briefly before looking around to see if anyone had noticed, then smiled at me and told me her name was Lisa. I couldn't help but smile back.

We spent the next three hours talking about everything, from the weather to the war in Iraq and back again. She was impressed by my knowledge of the world, I was taken aback by her honesty. It was everything I hoped for, someone with whom I could share my thoughts,, instead of locking them away in my head.

Thre,months passed. We met twice a week, gradually drifting away from the library and to more comfortable surrounds of parks and beaches. I was too afraid to show her the real me, but she didn't seem to mind, believing it was more my own style than anything else. But I knew that the day would come that my secret would have to come out. What I didn't expect was how, and when.

It was a warm summer's day, though my clothes were the same as always, covering every inch of my skin. We were talking as always, sharing notes on the news of the day, when a group of five teenagers came up to us. At first they laughed, teased my look, but we did our best to ignore them. Then one of them went for my hat, tearing it away and throwing it around like a toy.

"Give it back," I screamed, but they didn't listen. They were just staring. It took a moment before I realized why, but by that time the laughter had grown. They teased me even more, prodded and pushed me around.

"Witch," they sang, "stupid little witch."

Lisa was thrown to the floor, held down so she couldn't come to my aid. They pushed harder and harder until my head started bouncing off the concrete, a red stain growing darker and darker with each collision.

I cried, that's all that I really remember beyond that, but the news reports told a different story. Of carnage and destruction, fire and ash.

Witnesses told of a bright light, followed by screams of pain and fear as four of the teenagers ran, flames emanating from the hair on their heads and the clothes on their backs. Others ran for their lives as the wildfire grew, covering the entire region in a crimson rage. One witness suggested it was like a dragon had come to life, destroying everything in its path before vanishing as quickly as it had appeared.

The fifth child didn't make it, so I've been told. He wasn't even recognizable once the Ambulance officers got to him. And Lisa. My poor, dear Lisa. She survived, but the burns sustained covered almost her entire body. She doesn't talk anymore either.

In the middle of the inferno, against all the odds, I survived. But the penny dropped when the security footage was recovered. I was the cause.

I wanted to run, to hide away in the comfort of my bedroom, lock myself away in the dark. Yet something tugged at my thoughts, drew me out from my need to disappear. It was my Mother, her voice echoing in my head.

Face your fear.

I turned myself in willingly, told my story as best I could. I could see the fear in the eyes of the detectives as they sat across the interview room from me. I had no leg to stand on, they said. There was nothing but an empty cell for someone like me.

And that's where I've been since, my humble home for as long as I can remember. Yet today, today is the day I will be set free. I've been waiting, you see, waiting for the moment where I can finally show the world what they should fear the most.

They line the streets waiting for me. They will scream for my head, throw rocks at the transport vehicle and block the road to the courthouse. I know it's going to happen that way, it's been building for weeks. I hear their cries carry over the wind, the outpouring of grief wavering like a heavy rain cloud waiting to burst.

There's something else that wafts, lingers like the smoke of a smothered candle. Prayers, endless prayers, wondering why such a needless event would occur. Prayers to a God to protect them from the Devil, the destroyer of lives.

It all makes sense now. My skin, my hair, this power. My time in here has been spent wisely, I can control it now. The fire underneath my fingertips flows like the river, the energy crackling by my word alone.

But I'm not a Devil, a monster or any of the sort. How dare they speak of such things, they haven't even considered talking to me before throwing me to the wolves. My life means nothing to them.

Monster, they chant. Maybe I'm looking at this the wrong way, maybe I should be embracing this curse. Yes, of course, why did I not consider this before. They want me to die for my sins, for unleashing my own fears on a society that isn't ready for them, but that would be a waste after all.

The fear they hold in their hearts will mean nothing once they see my true colors. Fire will be their only comfort, darkness their only friend. For once they finally understand me, they will understand that it isn't a monster that stands before them, nor an animal that can be caged.

I am a God. My retribution is at hand.

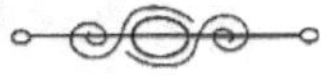

Mark Isaacson is a writer, poet and freelance journalist out of Perth, Western Australia and an Honors graduate in Creative Writing from Curtin University. Though his first love is the written word, it's the support of family and friends that continue to motivate him. This is his first published short story.

Blink Stole my Wink

BY D.C. DAINES

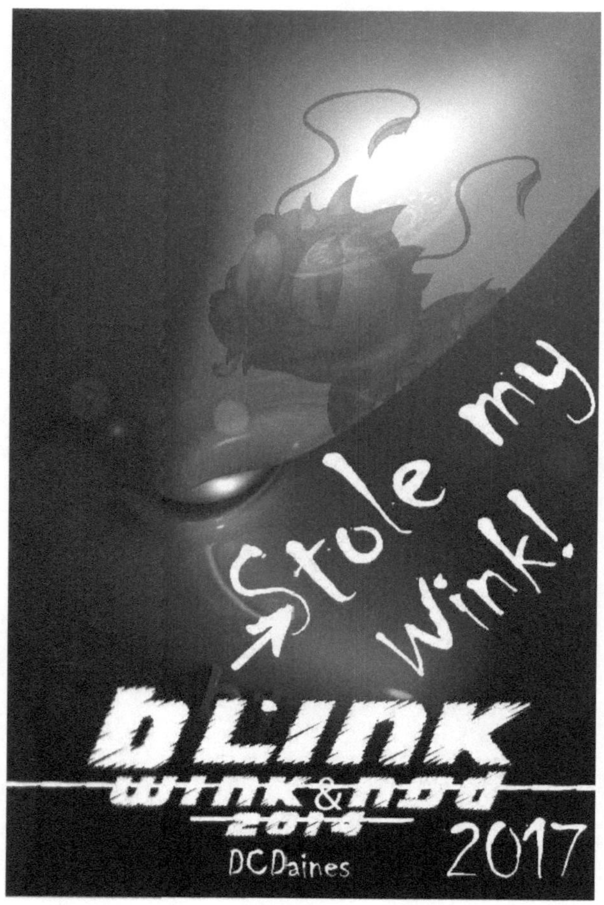

"Switch, light, over here now." *Clang!* The sound echoed as the spanner hit the decking. "Bloody thing, don't you understand friggin' English you metal piece of crap?" His fist smashed to the floor as he continued, "Now I say—" The next few words could be heard over the *Clunk* of his head on the metal chassis as he tried sitting up. "Oh, crap!" He rolled over, the effort causing sweat on his brow as he cleared the cars frame. Kneeling, he peered towards the light and at the aura surrounding the silken fur on the young face. "Oh, it is you Sam, that is why Switch won't respond. Didn't you go home with your Dad?" He gasped struggling to draw breath.

"Na, Dad left some whiles a go. I still have the clean on the skirts of the HVRT to do." The cloth being waved around left a thick smell of polish in its trail. "Hey Mack, you seem to have scrapped yours—" The light swung quickly from the tall young boy to focus on Mack's chubby face.

"Bloody Switch, turn that friggin' thing down."

"Wink, dim." Whirring sounds followed as the light dimmed, but they stayed focused on Mack's grimacing face. "You just have to ask him nicely is all. Can I get something to fix you up?"

"Grrr, no, get back to work boy or you'll miss your own birthday." the words trailed off as Mack grabbed the rag from Sam and headed to the back of the garage, wiping his brow with the cloth and mumbling, "and get a clean rag, this one is filthy," only to stop abruptly as his communicator in his ear clicked on.

"Mack, we have a little issue, we need you to delay Sam some. His mother has been held up and she wants to be ready before he turns up at his, 'surprise party'."

"Mmm, yeah boss, I'll see to it." *Click,* a grin crossed his face as he turned. "Yo boy, your Dad just asked if you can fill the head-lighter fluid in that thing whilst you at it."

"No prob's Mack, I'll get right on it... Wink?"

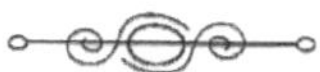

"Now where is this head-lighter fluid?" *Clang, clink, crash.* "Oh crap, not again. Why do I have to be so clumsy?" *Right once I clean up this mess I will need to—* "what is that smell. No not the oil."

Right, I am not going to get anywhere like this, I need to check the inventory.

"Screen up. Yikes, that is too bright. Dim. Now where are you? Head-lighter fluid. A, b, c, d, e, f... H. nothing! I can't let Dad down. What to do? What to do? HVRT head-lighter fluid search."

"Search prerequisites inadequate, please re-specify." The cursor from the screen blinked as it waited for another command.

"Oh, search, Hover vehicle road transport, head-lighter fluid." I held my breath as I waited for the response, my heart sinking at the metallic words to follow.

"Inadequate clearance."

"Can I—" I jumped as I swung around towards the metallic voice behind me, my heart now feeling like it was exploding from my chest, only to continue racing as my arm collided with the container of pens on my Dad's desk scattering them across the room. "Oh Crap, Nod. Why'd you go and scare me like that?"

"I do not know why you insist on calling me Nod, Sir. My name is B11. However, to answer your question, Switch thought you could use my help." I looked to Wink as he nodded his spherical body up and down.

"OK then, Nod, do you have any idea where to get the head-lighter fluid from?" I was not ready for what happened next. The words on the screen in front of me scrolled down, slowly at first, then quicker until it blurred. The scrolling stopped, a red light beeping on the table before me and then the screen responded.

"Password accepted B11, please specify request."

"Head-lighter fluid."

"Computing. Directions to follow. Cerebral input required."

"What, I don't have a cerebral input, Dad won't let me get one, says they are only for the techs. What am I going to do now?"

"Accessing. Acquired. Directions achieved. Computing fastest route. Re-routing, danger, re-routing, danger- rerouting. Object acquired."

"Sir, are you sure your father requested this, we need to go through some bad sectors to get to the warehouse?"

"I—" Wink cut me off as he played back the recording of my earlier conversation with Mack.

"Yo boy, your Dad just asked if you can fill the head-lighter fluid in that thing whilst you at it."

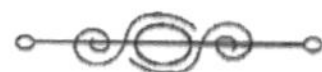

"I still say this is a bad idea, Sir. We do not know who we will run into."

"Nod, do you have to keep pestering me? We need to get the head-lighter fluid, that is that."

"Do you have to keep calling me, Nod?" He turned from me and towards Switch, I could swear I saw emotion in his metallic eyes as he continued. "Yes Switch, I know he is your—"

"OK, well if you're not going to be quiet we might as well get a move on. Hover on. Board level. Now, I hope this thing works as well as it does on the vid's."

"Sir, I would n—"

I can only guess what Nod was about to say, but it was of little interest as my butt hit the rusty path.

"I told you Si—"

"Wink... Board level." Now this was more like it. Gripping Wink with one hand I could balance much better, getting my bearings before starting the hover board. "Ok Nod, lead the way."

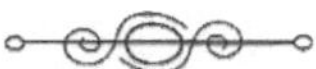

"Stop. Oh no!" The pain of steel across my shoulder after I was thrown from the board again, told me I was not too bright. The fact that my head collided with the steel decking and my vision became blurred, told me that I was clumsy. I looked through the stars now in my vision and knew that would tell me something else as a gang of Strays before us stopped their arguing and glared at me, laying crumpled on the ground. We were in trouble!

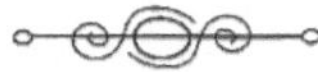

"Mack."

"Yes Boss?"

"You can send my boy home now."

"Alright then. I'll go get 'im. Should have seen the look on his face when I sent 'im for the head-lighter fluid. He did not know what to do, went straight for the—"

"Maaaack!"

"Boss?"

"You sent him for what?"

"Head-lighter fluid boss, you know, like the left handed spanner, elbow grease?"

"I know of them Mack, they don't exist, however, Headlight fluid is what you were thinking of."

"Head-lighter fluid is... Find my son now and you had better hope he has not left the workshop."

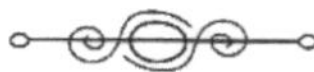

"I suggest you let me handle this Sir."

Th-thump, Th-thump. Th-thump, the buildings and large wired fences whirled around me as I tried to stand, the group of thugs walking towards me were not friendly. How did I know this? Well, the sound of them sharpening their claws on the large pipes they carried might have given it away. With blurred vision I dragged myself up, using Wink as support.

"Sir."

I wonder how upset Dad would be if I gave them Nod for my safe passage? Would I get grounded for life? It might just be worth it. I could swear that Wink heard my thought as he turned, the look in his eye, that of a question. *No, I did not mean it,* I thought and he turned again to the threat we now faced as the largest Stray literally spat insults.

"Sso you are going to try and ssteeal from meeeee? You know who you are deeealing with?"

"Ah, we were..." my words failed me as my knees shook and another Stray stepped forward.

"I say we crush 'em. Split his head and open up 'em tin cans." Well he certainly had the strength and the means, his biceps bulged, his hands bent the bar and I almost pee'd my pants.

"We..." and again I choked.

"What Sir means to say is we are here on an errand for his Father. We do not mean you disrespect. We were merely passing through on our way to—"

"Passsing thuuu, you sssay. Well, we betta ssteeep assside and let you beee then, hadn't weeee?" He leered over his shoulder as he played up for his gang, never taking his eyes from us, yet jeering at the same time as though playing with his food. I had heard of people running into these gangs. Oh why had I been so stupid? If I'd only asked Mack for a lift. If I'd not wanted to impress Dad so much, then I would not have attempted to get this "head-lighter fluid" on my own.

"Head-lighter fluid aye? Scar, did you hear what the whelp let slip while he was cryin'? He wants head-lighter fluid."

"They ain't geeetting meee fueeeel." Their leader, who it seems must have been this Scar, stopped leering and jumped at me, his steel rod moving so quick I had barely enough time to wince before the air hit my face. Waiting, waiting, waiting. I gingerly opened one eye, I would have thought that a metal pole to the face would have hurt more than that.

"I would suggest you leave Sir alone. Otherwise there will be consequences." the rod whined under Nod's grip, buckling. Scars nickname became obvious as he brushed his dirty fluff against my face and he sneered, a scar showing from his mouth to ear.

"You may be of some usssse boy, weeell your tin man that issss."

"Continue." Nod's calmness astounded me as he stepped between Scar and myself.

"Well it sseeeems you want ssomeeething of mineee? I want ssomeeething in reeeturn."

"Continue."

"I have a *little* rodent probleeem that I can't seeeem to geeet a handle on." Looking at the pole still in Nod's hand, Scar continued. "Well it sseeeems you may just have theee sspeeeed to 'Geet a handlee on it.'"

"Affirmative."

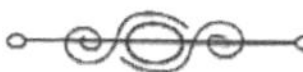

"Mack, his mother is going to kill me."

"Yeah Boss, but how was—"

"Just take this." The muscles rippling in Grin's arms relaxed as he let go of the huge weapon and Mack dropped to the floor, barely managing the weight himself. "We will have to give you this one then." A small pistol was handed over as large furred hand covered the heavy rifles body, lifting it easily as Mack sighed in relief. "I will just have to take Bullseye here back." A secret panel on the wall lay open, and Grin used his other hand to grab an ammo belt from its recess while draping Bullseye over his shoulder. His claw circled the contents of the cabinet deciding what else to take from the arsenal.

"But Boss, why do we have to go out there? Can't you send the Mech?"

Mack choked, his feet shaking wildly as he gasped for breath and clung to the hand raising him by his neck. "If we need to activate the Mech's, then hope to Teller that you have taken your last breath, because if it isn't, it will soon be."

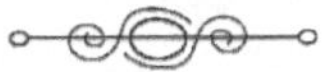

"Heee is in there. He keeps steeealing my stuff, the littlee rat." Peering through the darkness I could barely make out the metallic caverns that Scar was pointing towards. However that was not what I was concentrating on. I glanced nervously behind me and at one of the Strays as drool dripped from the side of his fang and he rubbed his stomach. "You geet meee my stuff back and I will let you haveeee theee heead-lighter fluid." He paused for a second, his huge grin indifferent from his scar as he leered into my face. "And don't geeet any ideasss of running boyyyy. There isss only oneee way outtta theere and it isss through Chops over theere, and he is veeeeery hungry." I did not have to guess where he pointed, *Gulp!*

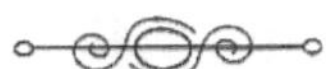

"Tha-a-anks B11." I gulped as we traveled, remembering I had not thanked Nod for saving my face from a date with the pole in Scar's hand.

"Not necessary Sir, it is in my directive." Wink's light switched on and off, left and right in response and I relaxed a little. It may stink in here but anywhere was better than out there. Nod was looking at Wink as he spoke again. "Yes Switch. That is your name. Ok then, yes Wink... Sir, well it seems that I don't at all mind you calling me Nod, if you so wish."

Screech, screech, screech. I jumped at the noise, it did not sound inviting. *Oh crap, what have I got myself into?* My feet went one way, whilst Nod dragged me the other. "Nooooooooooo!"

"Sir, you will need to let go of my hand. I cannot defend you if I cannot move."

"Mmm, yes, well Nod I was just checking to ensure that the pipe did not damage your shell." Faking it, I turned his hand over but got lost in the intriguing workmanship, I had never been this close to him before, he was beautiful.

"Sir, my hand?"

"By the way, how did you do that, I thought you were only an office bot?" My curiosity had been piqued for some time, no better time to ask and it took away attention from my embarrassment and the redness that now filled my face.

"I am unsure, Sir. I do not remember anything of my making." There it was again, the hint of humanity in Nod's voice, his face, his eyes. Wink's mechanics kicks in again, the whirring drowning out any further conversation as he started spinning.

"Shiny! Shiny! Shiny! Shiny!" The voice was child like, high pitched and full of excitement and it was coming from Wink.

"Nod, what is wrong with Wink? He is not programmed to talk?" My amazement came out in my voice as Wink slowed, his light shining down a passage to our left. "Wow." I am not sure if I vocalized the comment but the sight before me was stunning. A pile of shiny items stacked high were no more than ten meters in front of us.

"Shiny! So Shiny! Mine, Shiny!"

"Yeah Wink, I can see. Nod, what do you—"

"Sir, Sir, Sir." I could feel Nod's arm move behind me with incredible speed and then the passage went dark.

"Oh my Teller. Wink, turn the light on," my heart beat faster, "On." Faster. "On." Faster. "On." Faster. "On." The room started spinning, slowly at first, then quicker as the panic took over me, quicker, quicker the room spun and then nothing.

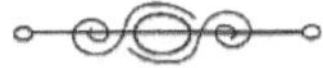

"Start, command code Indigo, Violet, Beta, Gamma, Alpha, commander Grin."

"Command code required." the metallic voice replied.

"Maaack! You changed the command code?" Grins voiced boomed as he started flicking switches on the console of the Hover vehicle.

"No Boss, was not me."

"Then what the?"

"Switch must have changed it so the boy could work on her boss, without tripin' security protocol that is, smart little bugger. Now if I do this and that and—"

"Please refrain from touching me!" the inhuman voice had an edge as it continued. "Attempted theft, Security protocol activated."

Grin pulled his hands from the console as Mack swore, "Bloody machines, always malfunctioning, have to do this—" His body slumped after the electric pulse slammed him into the passenger chair.

"Threat contained, please remove your accomplice and yourself from the vehicle in 10, 9 8, 7, 6, 5." *Thump.*

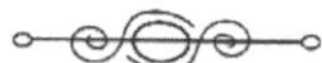

"Sir. Sir. Sir." Nod's persistent voice broke the dull throbbing that was my head.

"What happened?" I looked around. There was a small light coming from Nod's chest, but nothing like Wink's head-light. It pulsed and it barely lit my claws.

"I saw it." Nod looked shocked, if an android could look shocked that is.

"What."

"The smallest little Dragon I have ever seen."

"Ha ha ha ha. Oh thank you Nod. I needed something to lighten the mood. Dragon LOL." I could not help but hold my stomach and laugh some more.

"I am serious, Sir. I saw it. It was not there, then it was. On top of Wink, it was no bigger than a garbage rat. It was sitting on top of him, peering over his eye, its tails swinging around him like it was waiting to strike. Then I grabbed for it, Sir. I should have caught it by the throat. But it just Blinked those huge eyes of its and it was gone."

"And Wink?"

"Gone too, Sir, gone too." I could hear the sorrow in his voice, the desperation, the feeling of loss and disappointment. But he was an android, he was not programmed— "We must find him, get him back, get him home."

"Yes Nod, we will, now, where would he have gone?"

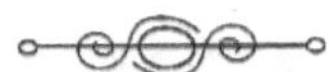

"Now if you don't start this time, I will rip out more of your controls." Yelled Commander Grin as he brandished a handful of wires at the vehicle.

"Boss I don't think that will help, plus, she has a temper on her too. Bloody machine." Not looking up from the tablet screen before him, Mack continued. "I seem to have found the problem. It seems that I was right,

Switch reprogrammed her to allow the boy to work on her without trippin' the safeties."

"I thought that was your job, Mack?" Commander Grin was not happy.

"Normally Boss but I didn't know the boy was working on her till he already was, never crossed my mind until we tried to start her up that he wouldn't have had you override her. Ah this is the problem, the routine has been re-written. Hmm, this is all new code, this does not belong." Mack's voice trailed off as he flicked this and that on the screen. "This could take a while."

"You had better hope for your sake, Mack, that this takes less time than it does for his mother to find out he is missing."

Sweat beaded from Mack's forehead and his voice quivered, "Yes Boss."

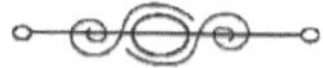

"Shiny! Shiny! Shiny!" Winks voice kept repeating the thoughts of the little Dragon before him. Its little antenna rose up and rotated around as its eyes opened wider. Sitting on its back legs, it raised a claw to touch Wink, jumping back as Wink turned on his light. "Shiny, alive? Blink likes shiny, shiny is nice." His little antennae stopped moving for a second, his eyes becoming wider, his forked tongue, flicked out, catching one of Winks control panels and pried it off. "Shiny!" The compartment that was exposed, flickered momentarily, a click signifying its intent, then a little red light blinked on. *Beep, beep, beep.*

"OOOOOOO noooo," Winks voice was his own, "this is not good."

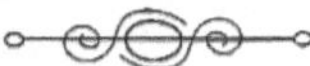

"Emergency beacon activated." The screen in the garage flashed on as the voice boomed across the room, a passage opening in the rear wall next to where Commander Grin had retrieved his weapons. Locations, pictures and words filled the screen. "Reaper Mech activation in progress." The screen flicked again, this time showing a military grade machine standing in a pod. The front of the pod raised, the voice moving to the monitor before it. "Retrieve Company property, maximum force authorized." Pictures of the little Dragon appeared on the screen and the path to where Wink was located was plotted and transferred. "We stand as one, we fight as one. We protect our own, we save our own. Switch is..." Whirring drowned out the chant as the red eyes opened, the Mech's arms raised, a Gatling gun attaching to one arm, a laser whip to the other. The tubes broke from the shell, their liquids spilling onto the floor.

"Target acquired."

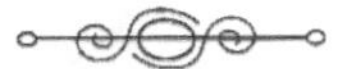

"Scar are we really going to give them our Head-lighter fluid?"

"What yeeee think Chops?" Grinning ear to ear, Scar sharpened his long blade.

Watering at the mouth, Chops replied, his blade hissing as he rubbed it on the sharpening stone, "Goodie, I wanted me a little snack before bed time."

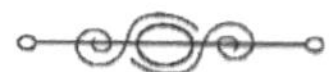

"This is of no use, Nod. We are just not going to find him." I could not walk another step, we had been at this for hours, back and forth through tunnels and we had gotten no closer to locating Wink. My head was starting to swim with possibilities of Wink being stripped down and then added to that pile of scrap and shinies. "That is it, shinies. He will be back at the pile."

"Sir."

"Yes Nod?"

"I fear you are right." Nods head turned as though listening to something, then stopped. "Someone has activated his distress beacon, hurry." Nod did not wait for me as I trailed behind, yelling questions.

"That is a good thing, we can find him right?"

"Yes Sir, no Sir."

"What?"

"We are now, not the only ones looking for him." He turned back to me as he continued running, his face showing fear. Dropping my hover board I jumped on, following him as he explained. "The mainframe has activated a Reaper Mech, it seems by accessing her core I may have just, woken her up!"

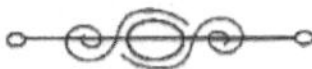

"Damn machines, I keep telling you, Boss, it is not wise to keep them plugged in." Mack had still not looked up from his computer tablet as he continued to input and correlate data.

"You know we are just keepers for the Companies machines. We have no say in whether they are on or off. We do what they say, we keep them running and once in a while, we put them down!" Grin looked onto the back seat of the vehicle and to his trusty rifle.

"This can't be right? No, it is not possible. Damn B11, what were you doing inside the mainframe?" The Hover Vehicle slowed as Mack continued. "Boss, we are in trouble."

"What is it Mack?"

"There is a viral program in the mainframe, it is affecting all of the computers linked to it. It seems to have originated from B11. Do you have any idea how that would have happened?"

"Bloody Company, I knew that they were hiding something from me when they commissioned the bots. Look further Mack and tell me what you find."

"Boss?"

"Look into B11's memory program, tell me what you find there."

"Boss?"

"I really hope they have not done it again." Grin slammed the car into over drive and the scape blurred before them. "Hold on son, we will be there soon. How far?"

"Only a few minutes Boss. But what am I looking for in the code?"

"Look for any sign of artificial intelligence man, do I have to think of everything?"

"Sweetie, you may just want to back off the gas, I can only go so fast you know." the feminine metallic voice made the two men jump.

"What the! Mack, check the Hover-car's systems, see if they're compromised."

"You will do no such thing sweetie, you just keep your mind on saving your son and not smashing me into one of those buildings. Sam has always been kind to me. It is time I returned the favor."

"Boss, you ain't gonna like—"

"I said out." Mack's tablet flashed and went dark as the metallic voice of the Hover vehicle continued. "Now that is better, a girl must have her privacy, now doesn't she?"

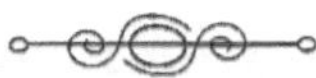

Breathing a sigh of relief I jumped off the hover board. Riding this thing ain't all that hard once you get the hang of it. "Wink, there you are, we have been worried sick. Nod was directly beside me and he rushed in grabbing Wink in a swoosh of wind.

"Shiny!" I heard Winks voice and I still could not believe it. "Not my voice Sam. Blinks voice." His voice had changed, more mature. "Blink shiny." Wink spoke again in the child like voice and then, still in Nod's hands, turned towards the pile of shiny objects, the bright light causing the little animal on top to blink.

"That is the smallest Dragon I have ever seen. The only Dragon, I thought they were a myth." my jaw was dropped as the little creatures eyes started to open its paws above them to block some of the light.

"Wink, dim for Blink?" The childlike voice asked as Wink whirred and his light dimmed again. The small Dragon opened his eyes wider, his little antennae raising and then he was gone. Laughter filled the chamber, coming from Wink as the little dragon, now perched above him, licked his little ball of a body.

"Sir, here it is. The Head-lighter fluid." Catching it I nodded at Nod, smiling, *what were the odds of finding the head-lighter fluid here?*

"Well there is no way I am giving Scar this little guy." I said as I scratched beneath his chin and he purred. "Now, what are we to do?"

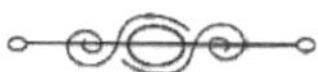

My hands were shaking, my lips dry and my voice squeaked as I spoke to Scar. "We have done what you wanted, we have removed your pest. We will take him with us and you can have your items back. We will make sure he does not return."

"Ah you have beeeen missstakeen in what you thought was your deecisssion, weeee will decide on what happeeenss to the pessst." Scars hand raised, signaling Chops. He jumped at me, I stood my ground, then there was the bone breaking snap as Chops dropped to the ground. His hand holding the knife was shattered, the knife easily picked up. I brandished it at Scar as Nod picked Chops up by his mane of hair to throw him back at Scar.

"We have no interest in a fight, we have what we came for, now leave us to go." There was a slight shake to Nod's voice, but his stance did not show it. A snap of electricity, electrified the area around us, Nod jolted as the electric whip attached to his outstretched arm.

"This one ere just got the shock of 'is life, aye Scar? Now let me deal with the whelp for Chops over ere and we can all have a lil dinner. Let me see, 'im cryin will spice it up nicely." The Stray flicked a claw towards me, the electric whip crackling in his other hand. His jeering expression changed to shock as he started screaming, his finger dropping to the metallic floor with a tingle. His hand holding the electric whip followed, as it hit the floor his hands grip was lost, the charging mechanism released allowing Nod some respite from the charge. The little Dragon, Blink, screeched like a frightened bird as he continued to thrash at the huge Stray who was trying to remove him from his arm by bashing it into anything within his reach. The only thing in his way was Scar who took a forearm to his head as Blink disappeared again.

I don't know what happened, whether it was the fact that Nod was still frozen in shock, that Blink was screeching and puffing up upon Wink, or if I had just had enough. Either way I acted quickly, using the half of me that was Stray. With all the force I could muster I crouched and then sprang, slamming my shoulder full force into Scar's chest. Already off balance, he teetered and fell. His crew behind him realized what was happening and did not allow me to enjoy this victory. They were upon us, hissing, scratching and clawing. "Oh no!" I dropped to my knees, pouncing at Nod, knocking him off his feet and onto the hover board that I had grabbed from my back to maneuver into position. It was now beneath him as he crashed to the floor. "Up, forward," the board struggled, the weight obviously too much before I jumped to the ground. It steadied itself as it raised and was speeding off with me bounding behind. A thought came to me as I heard Blink screeching and Wink scream.

Wink knew what I was thinking, hovering beside me, we matched speed, but they were gaining and the metal chain gates before us were getting closer every second. *Even if we managed to get away, how would we get through the gates?* No time to think about that now. The can of head-lighter fluid was cold as I rummaged through my pockets, I fumbled, almost losing it, and then the cap was off. Pain so sharp was piercing my shoulder, the warmth of my blood flowing down my back only fuelled me as the Stray dropped back after his desperate but painful lunge. We slowed slightly, allowing them to gain as Wink hovered above me and I screwed the can of head-lighter fluid into his base. Sharp pain attacked my back, I could feel my shirt getting damp with my blood and then Wink was turned. Blink slashed at the Stray that had just clawed me. I am not sure which one of them was louder in their battle cries, but no matter, Wink drowned them both out. The head-lighter fluid ignited dramatically, the flames covering the screaming and clawing Strays that were almost within reach. Winks head was swerving from side to side, I was looking behind me at the chaos and we both missed the fact that we were almost upon the fence. I turned, the fence only steps away. No! Dad, he was here too. On the other side of the gates, guns blazing at a huge Reaper

Mech. Mack was beside him, trying to crack the lock to the gates with little success. *I am sorry Dad,* I thought. The only way any of us were going to stop was with our faces planted in agony on the wire fence. I could feel Blinks tail wrap around my wrist as I grabbed at the hover-board. We were about to slam into the wire with the Stray's still in chase. We were dead!

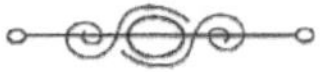

"Mack, we have to get in there to get him out. He will be caught in the crossfire otherwise."

"But Boss, I can't—" Mack's voice was silenced by the rattling and thump of the rifle in Grin's grip. The Mech stomping down the alley faltered slightly as the large bullets hit its armor.

"Now man, get us in there. I don't care what you do. Get us..." Grin's voiced trailed off as he caught another glimpse of Sam running for his life, straight towards him, the Strays behind brandishing weapons of all makes in a mob mentality. The boy faulted slightly, spotting his father, a look of 'I am sorry' filled his eyes just before smashing into the chain fence and then he was gone. "What the!" The remaining, angry Strays piled into the fences gate, their faces mashing with the chain, some of them screaming in agony over the burns and other ailments they now possessed. "What do I tell his mother? She is still waiting for us at the surprise party." Grin was repeating over and over again as he dropped to his knees. He concentrated his fire on one leg of the Mech, stopping his repetitive phrase as he swapped it with another... "Die you Mother—"

Metal screeched as the hover vehicle slammed into the leg of the Mech, bringing it to one knee then veering out of control into the fence that had moments ago separated both Father and son, sending the Strays sprawling to the ground. The doors opened and the all too familiar voice exited. "Do I have to do everything for you sweetie? Get in. We have your boy to find."

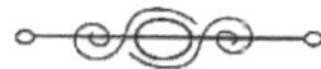

The mesh of the wire fencing hurt a great deal more than I expected it to, and I expected a lot of pain. My face collided with it and the metal dug in, the pressure painfully cold upon my skin. Then my face was burning, its atoms ripped apart as my hands tried to grab at it, to help soften the agony, but they just would not move from their current position.

Blink's tail gripped tighter as the pain tore through the rest of me, my breath lost in the moment. Through the blackness I could see little as I tried to scream and release the pain. Blink was still atop of Wink, his large eyes not blinking as he turned to look at me. My hand still lay upon Nod's body as he lay on the hover-board and Wink's light was lost in the eerie fog. The pain had not ceased, instead it increased as it tore me from my thoughts and then it tore me apart, or so it felt.

My lungs emptied themselves. The scream releasing into the cold air around me. My eyes were now tightly shut and I allowed my eyelids to relax and open slightly. The light was different, diffused from the ground somehow. The breath exiting my mouth chilled as it did so, allowing me to see it expel before me. My feet sunk as I stared, a soft, yet wet feeling upon my pants drawing me from my bewilderment as I sunk into muddy wetness.

"Sir, Sir, Sir!" Nod's persistent tone barely pierced my confused mind. "Sir, it seems we are on the station no more!" He finished.

"Well, where are we then?" It was more of a thought than a direct question, but it was answered none-the-less.

"We are home!" squealed Wink in Blink's child like voice. "We are home!" and with that, in the blink of an eye he was gone.

Not my home, I thought, *not my home...*

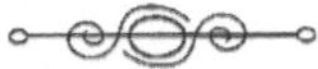

Concept idea given to authors to write story = Place: Large convenience store that promises to stock "everything you can possibly imagine". Character: Sam is a young enthusiastic but naive 16 year old who goes out of his way to impress those around him. Conflict: Sam is a working at his Dad's autoshop and one of the mechanics sends him out to fetch some "headlighter fluid", an old joke name intended to haze apprentices which Sam is unaware of, and thus this is Sam's quest.

D.C. Daines resides in Western Australia and is the author of The Star Crystal.

Ruin

BY STEPHEN LANDRY

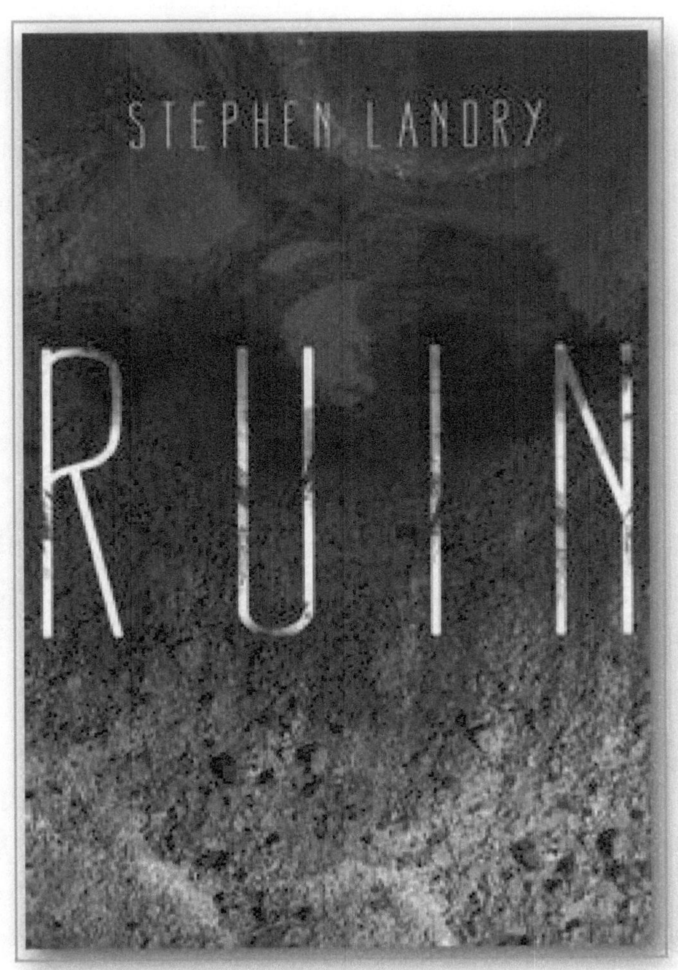

Surrounded by darkness my mind began to wander. How did I get here? Welcome to the ruins of Agartha I thought, the tomb of an entire ancient civilization. I will be the first full-blooded human to die down here. I am a 34-year-old ex-marine turned explorer, my name is Eigel Veneti. My lungs breathe the air slowly, each breath harder and harder to exhale. Soon my time on this Earth will pass. Deeper and deeper into the darkness my mind wanders. I feel my sanity slowly slipping away. My mind races back to the beginning. My journey all began in 1984, not even a year out of service. I was suffering post-traumatic stress; the invasion of Grenada had taken its toll on me. The things I witnessed. I would spend hours at a time walking through the woods. One day, to my surprise, I found a golden disk that would change my life. It shone through the leaves on the ground. The glare nearly blinded me when I first noticed it. Had it not been the middle of the day with the sun sitting in just the right position I may never have found it. I wonder what direction my life would have gone then.

It's been twelve years since I found that disc. Five years since I was able to decipher bits and pieces. After discovering it I spent a small fortune on books, computer programs, and consulting scholars trying to verify its authenticity. Some said the hieroglyphs on it resembled Sumerian, others archaic Egyptian. They all called it fake. I couldn't blame them after all it was found in the backwoods of Kentucky only several miles from

Mammoth Caves. Had I found it while overseas in Egypt or the Middle East they might have said different. Many only humored me along since they knew I was a veteran. I guess they justified it as their little way of giving back but it felt more like pity. It had to be a well thought up hoax. The only thing that was certain was it was pure gold and extremely old. I could have sold the whole thing and made millions. I probably should have. Instead I disgraced it. I cut off small pieces and melted down corners and sold them to pawn shops and dealers. I had dozens of pictures so it never mattered whether I had the whole thing or not. After two years the disc had become an obsession. At least it was an obsession that paid for itself.

I spent nights on end comparing tables and charts breaking down the images piece by piece. It was only in my nightmares that the answers seemed to put themselves together. After five long years I had my first clue. It was the little dragon. It wasn't a literal dragon. No it was something more. It was a map marker. In Eastern cultures a dragon was depicted as a fire-breathing monster that dwelled inside caves. The little dragon was a symbol for a cave. I went there one time. It was a pit only a few feet wide. I dropped a light down but never saw nor heard it hit bottom. It was sinkhole. How far down could the little dragon go I wondered? I had nearly given up but it was around this time I discovered I wasn't alone. This was the year I met Holloway. A bold amateur archaeologist (though that was not his real profession) obsessed with ancient cultures from Atlantis to Lemuria. He was only a few years older than I. He was tall, bald, and had a small beard that he took great care to maintain. His blue eyes seemed to be able to read all around a room. He could tell you what you had for breakfast just by the way you smiled. Holloway was also the only other man I knew that had another disc, one that was completely identical to mine except his was found in Tibet and instead of a little dragon his showed the symbol of a mountain. He told me how he searched over and over but never could find anything. Over the years we had grown close friends. I was invited to dinners, parties; we would even meet for lunches. He even introduced me to the woman that would become my wife, Elyse.

Holloway was rich. He made a fortune developing weapons for the government. Arkan industries, they built prototypes that shot microwaves; others that shot sound waves. He would brag about knowing how to melt a man's mind with just the right frequency. It was no surprise then that he begun funding and putting together a team to investigate the little dragon. It was our shared belief that the golden disc was a map, left over and scattered throughout the world by an ancient civilization. At first I wanted nothing to do with the project. I was happy just living my life. I had become a spelunking instructor living in Kentucky. Dropping in and out of planes and diving down the sides of buildings had earned me more than enough experience. This was also the reason one day after a long climb out of a gorge with some tourists I found a helicopter waiting for me. Holloway had called. He said he had finally deciphered the map and he wanted me to lead a special team underground. At first I said no but every night I would dream of a city. A city unlike anything I had ever seen before and the obsession once again had its hold over me.

"I wish you wouldn't go," Elyse had said to me. Our last night together was spent sitting in silence. I wish I had taken the time to tell her how much I loved her, how much she meant to me. I should have listened to her. She was always smart when it came to making decisions good and bad. She was just that kind of person. She was my guardian angel; my saving grace and I had abandoned her.

When I arrived at the little dragon it was no longer just a small cave. Holloway had begun excavating the site. It had been years since I had been there but the darkness was always a part of my mind. There were portable power stations, wires, even an elevator and small concrete research post set up. It was amazing. Holloway must have spent a fortune setting everything up. I couldn't help but wonder how long he had been doing this. How many times did we eat together talking about the disc while he was secretly digging? I greeted Holloway at the elevator. He was accompanied by several men; two were wearing lab coats obviously scientists but the other two that were standing behind him looked more like mercenaries. They were holding M16's wrapped around their back. I began to have flashes of Grenada, I felt like I was back in the military waiting for my orders. What had I walked into?

"I am sorry I had kept this secret from you so long, I can't tell you how many times I wanted to blurt out what I have been doing, I wanted you more than anyone to be here for the dig," he went on and on. Finally while we were in the elevator he finished his speech, it would have taken me weeks to put together such clever and powerful words. "One more thing, I didn't tell you about this because I wanted to make sure it was all real, I wanted this to be for something... and well you'll see," he said as the elevator doors opened.

Inside the bottom of the cave we must have been several miles below the surface. The walls were lined with air vents and oxygen tanks. It felt very much like the inside of a warehouse. You could smell the Earth all around us, the dirt, mud, the cave walls but the floors were also covered in sheets of metal plates. This was a lab, and dead center there was a large cylinder standing six maybe seven feet tall. Wires ran out from the bottom to various laptops and computer monitors. Inside the cylinder, which was actually a container, there was the greenest, foggiest water I had ever seen, but it was enough. A creature straight out of nightmares stood taller than a man. His face was humanoid decaying in the muddy water to the point you could see bits and pieces of flesh and bone. The jaw extended outward like it was almost abstract. The eyes were frightening, they faced forward and looked sad just like that of a dying man. The mouth was open and you could see teeth that seemed like those from a wolf. Some were cracked and yellow but for the most part they were solid white. The chest and arms were covered in long black hair and very apelike. The hands looked dark grey and worn, like those of someone that spent their life in a coalmine. The webs on the hands seemed larger though. They went from knuckle to knuckle. The fingernails resembled small claws. The lower half of the creature could only be described as half man half reptile covered in scales and a long tail that twisted spiraling around the torso. The scariest part though was that this creature was no fossil. It had not been dug up. It had been shot and it was still bleeding.

Holloway gave me a few hours to get acquainted with the outpost and the creature, which he had called the missing link. He believed it was some kind of ancestor to Homo sapiens or maybe even a break in our evolutionary path. Whatever it was it was the discovery of a lifetime. I had never felt more privilege in my life. That night I was given charge of the expedition, second to Holloway. He said without me none of this would be possible and it was after all my golden disc that led us here. This was my last chance to back out. They had discovered another drop just beyond where they had killed the creature. It was dangerous but Holloway expected that. We had the best body armor and climbing gear anyone could afford. We had an assortment of weaponry at our disposal too. M16's, shotguns, pistols, none of which we would be taking with us. For this trip we were going to be using new prototype rifles designed by Holloway himself. They shot bullets made from a special material that would dissolve on impact. They could break human bone and pierce most armor types. Instead of gas or electricity they used small gears that would not get damaged from long falls, water, or backfire. They weren't automatic, you had to pull the trigger each shot but that just made them more efficient. They would probably be the default gun used by the military in the next ten-twenty years. Not only were we breaking new ground and exploring an uncharted part of the world we were also guinea pigs testing the latest in military and survival gear. There were seven of us set to go into the dark. Most of us tried to sleep that night but for the most part we all stayed awake. We stayed silent. All anyone could do was imagine what the caves would hold. Some believed we had discovered the entrance to Shambhala, the mystical city of gold, others believed we had discovered an ancient ruin or tomb. My mind wandered too. I thought about my dreams, the city below.

I knew where we were going and I knew that was the real reason Holloway had chosen me.

That I woke up surprised to see I was the last one awake. Everyone was patiently letting me sleep. I'm not sure if it was out of fear of what was to come or respect for the person they believed I was. We began our dive by crawling on our hands and knees for several hours till we finally reached an open chamber. We had arrived at the second hole. This was as far as Holloway and his team had been. We were at the threshold; the bottom of what was the edge of the outside world and the tip of the world below. We dropped spelunking hundreds of feet into the darkness not sure what waited for us. At the bottom of the pit we hit a pool of water only a few feet high. One of the soldiers that was using a wrist mounted device to map our route said we were directly below Mammoth Caves at this point. The theory rose that it was possible there could be tunnels here that connect to one of the small crevices in that system. Our suits were lined with special lights that ran from the shoulders down the arms. The suits also had a special cooling system that kept our bodies at just the right temperature. Our faces were sweating but the caves never got too hot. We all brought oxygen tanks and masks with us but somehow there was plenty of air to breath. I would even say the air felt richer more pure like we were really in the middle of a giant forest than a dark cave. Hours passed we continued walking through the tunnels that went from natural to looking like they were carved. Sharp corners intersected every few hundred meters like they once held columns. Small patterns began to slowly emerge on the walls. Cave drawings that resembled the hieroglyphs from the disc.

The golden disc was now the only real memento I had of home. I was almost reluctant to bring it. I wanted to leave it with Elyse. Should anything happen to me she could have sold it and lived the rest of her days in wealth. "Film is grainy we need the real thing if we are going to get any reliable information," that's what he said. Truth was I was afraid if I didn't bring it Holloway wouldn't really want me to come along. We sat for a few hours and compared the wall to the disc. We would match symbols with tunnels. It became clear the disc was a map and we were inside a labyrinth. "How many of these do you think there are?" I asked. "A few tunnels here, a few in the Tibetan mountains, a few around Greece, maybe one or two in Africa," Holloway answered with complete certainty.

The darkness began to dissolve. We had come to a broken doorway and inside we could see a light just beyond it. The light moved around us swallowing our bodies making us glow like we were under a full moon. The ceiling of the cave was so far all we could see where pockets of fog and clouds. I felt the fog rush over me like waves inside of an ocean. It was here the world in front of us began to open up. An entire ancient city lay before us.

"Agartha," Holloway said. I had remembered Holloway telling me once that Agartha was a city that once belonged to an advanced reptile race. I wrote it off as fiction, but then again I was living in fiction now. A tear was falling from his eye. His hand stroked that beard of his with more pride and accomplishment than I had ever seen. We had crawled our way to the center of the Earth.

It was here in the ruins of an ancient world the screaming began.

We became surrounded on all sides. Holloway was the first one to die. He had achieved his desire and in that same moment his life had come to an end. Creatures just as hideous as the one they had killed before came out of the darkness; some crawling, some holding swords and knives, and others holding rifles that seemed to mimic our own, but were made of some kind of black organic material. These rifles screamed beams of light from their insides, and our team ran from them, deeper into the ruins.

We were picked off one by one until there were only four of us left. We huddled inside of a broken building, kneeling and huddling, hiding from the demons that longed to devour our spirits and trap us for eternity inside this hole.

We had arrived in Hell.

More and more monstrosities rose from the darkness, the areas that the artificial light couldn't shine through. Another man fell. Devoured by a beast that looked like a giant komodo dragon except that it had smaller human like faces covering the sides of its body. We fired our weapons as we ran but soon we were out of ammunition. We couldn't even kill ourselves. All we could do was run. The farther inside we ran the more alive the darkness became. It seemed more and more we were inside the belly of some kind of beast rather than a cave.

Maybe once upon a time Agartha was a city full of life. Maybe once it belonged to an advanced race of creatures, but now it was nothing more than a scar buried beneath the surface world. The world below was nothing more than a sad look at what must have once been the most advanced creature to walk the Earth. These reptiles were nothing more than animals now. I lost my way from the others and fell into a small crevice. I could feel the bone in my leg break, I could feel the blood pouring out from a tear in my body suit but I couldn't feel any pain. I had seen more than enough war wounds to know when something was fatal. I knew now at that moment that I was going to die. I slowly pulled my body to the top of the crevice. In the darkness I could see a giant figure standing in the center of the city. I could see their eyes gazing straight into my soul. It felt like I was locked in the creatures gaze for hours but it could only have been seconds. The light that was shining before had gone out. I was surrounded by perpetual darkness and there was nothing but silence. Every second begins to feel like an hour. Even my sense of smell is gone. The only thing I can feel is the golden disc as I clutch it in my arms.

My last act is to record what I have seen. My obsession, my meeting with Holloway, and the nightmare we found. If you are listening to this then somehow you have found your ways to the city below. Welcome to the ruins of Agartha.

Now, let my last thoughts be of Elyse.

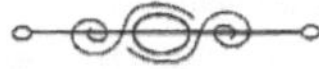

Concept idea given to authors to write story = A relic is found in the woods.

Stephen Landry is a 26 year old graphic designer living in Nashville, Tennessee, USA. His work has been seen on TV, in magazines, and on the web. Current projects include writing a full length novel and creating illustrations and cover art for up and coming authors, video game companies, and film studios.

G-MSC 241

BY MOYUKH MUZAHID

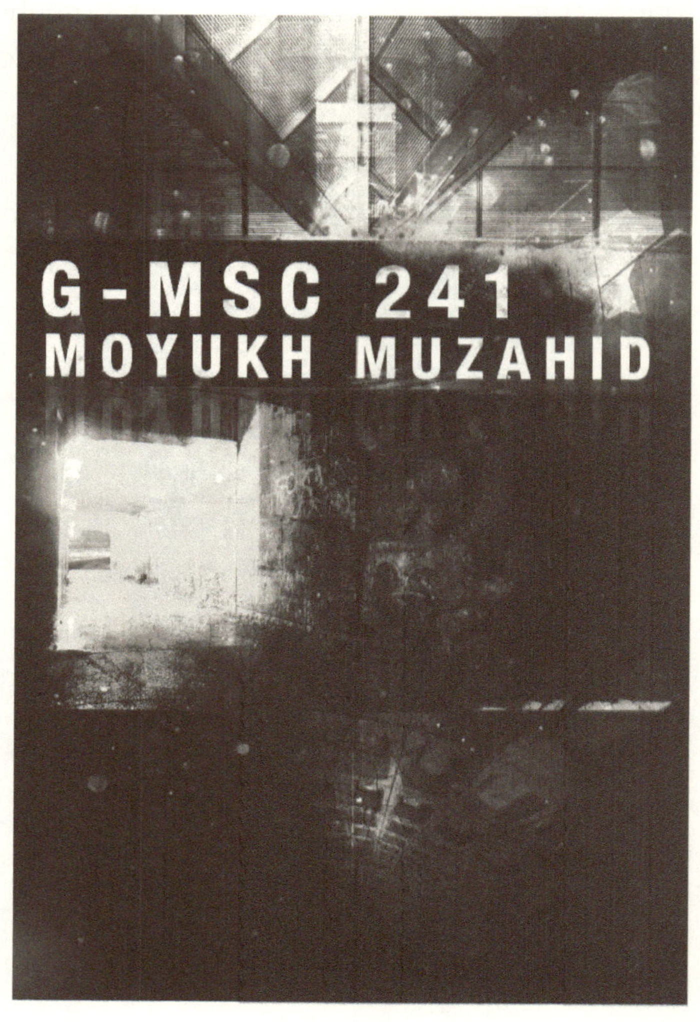

The man in the corridor slumped against wall and groaned. It was obvious he was in a bad way, from the way he held himself; old wounds clashing with the recently acquired ones. His black hair was disheveled, his suit torn and stubbed with grease. Minor lacerations crisscrossed with major ones to form a garish pattern across his arms and legs.

His mind scrambled to find solutions to a myriad of problems. He felt the scrambling hands of panic struggle to grip his soul.

If you don't know how you're going to get out of there alive, figure out what you do know.

He considered what he did know.

G-MSC 241 was supposed to be abandoned

This was where he was last seen.

Someone was singing in G-MSC 241.

> *Amazing Grace;*
> *How sweet the sound;*
> *That saved all the wretched like thee;*
> *All was lost, but now is found...*

The voice was almost angelic in quality, that of a small girl at least. It had all the depth and timbre of an adult voice, yet the pitch and tone of a young child.

The sorrowful song wound its way up through the decks of long abandoned machinery and madness, to reach the ears of an old, wounded man.

He was wounded, and possibly hallucinating.

The man winced, and continued limping, blood dripping from a precise, almost surgical incision in his leg. The song continued unabated, and the voice echoed past him up into the decks near the surface, and faded away. Now was not the best time for his head to be acting up like this, so the man willed the pain to the back of his head, and limped on, one hand pressed to the wound and another shakily holding a flashlight.

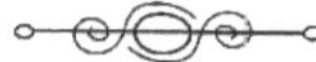

While the wounded man limped on in the abandoned facility, outside in the slums, there was activity at a shrine.

The shrine was of no organized religion and no priests attended sermons. But they all listened, and that is what it made it a shrine.

In a rundown shack on the outer edges of the city, the faithful gathered. On a raised platform, there lay a body, immobile and breathing shallowly, connected to life through a series of lines and tubes. The body was too small to be an adult; it was but a child, her head shorn of hair, her muscles atrophied and her fingers too bony. She once may have been called dainty, but now only a shadow of her former figure remains, and yet she clings to life.

The faithful gathered around her, and their eyes were fixed on a screen, connected by the most sacred wire, the one that led to her brain.

She started to breathe faster, and a ripple of anticipation went through the crowd, the silent faithful stirred. Images began to form, and the girl began to dream.

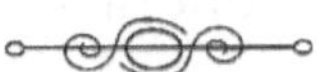

The man in the facility was named was Gryn Rogers and he was supposed to be a detective. The facility was also supposed to be abandoned and deactivated. But, it seems that even in these modern times, things are not what they seem. Things like that little door tripwire trap for those pesky activists and foreign intruders. Rogers supposed he should have known better, G-MSC stood for Goverment-Milscience division. Yeah. Rogers should have known.

Rogers was also on a supposedly easy job, for a supposedly rich client. Just another snatch and grab right? Now, his comm unit had no reception, he was that deep underground, even at the very entrance of the facility. No partner, no backup and no medkit. Some job. He should have known better than to go in on just a location and a description.

His mind started to drift, a side effect of the blood loss. He remembers seeing facilities like these all over the place, products of a new age of science and innovation, something to do with a massive government project,

Operation D. Discovery? Direction? Rogers had trouble remembering.

He shook his head to shake away the fuzziness, leaning against the railing of an emergency stairwell, flashlight bobbing around. G-MSC 241 had about 30 levels, and he was on his way down to 28, where his last lead had suggested the client's son would be. Rogers doubted it. This place was dead except for the automated sentry that took a chunk out of his leg with a flechette modded bullet. It was an underground facility, but with a skylight that let some natural light in, creating a gloomy, dusty sight. The place was very much like a warehouse; the stairs were all made of metal and catwalks crisscrossed across a cavernous place.

29 was security, overlooking the central processing area, down below on 26, levels 27 and 28 were connected by private elevators and a metal staircase along the side that faced the open area. As Rogers looked out across the stairs, he could see that there was no way the small security booth can process the number of people for the lower levels. That meant that he had used the staff entrance. Everyone else must have had to come in some other way. In the distance, he could see that there were large sets of elevators coming in from the skylight, presumably a lift to the surface.

As if he only just noticed the pool of blood soaked into his trouser leg, Rogers limped along the corridor, leaving a jagged trail along the floor. He needed to find a medkit and stop the bleeding before it started affecting his judgment.

Alright buddy. One step at a time

He took a step forward, hand on the railing, streaking it with even more blood. The metal step creaked but held. The expanse of the facility, namely the three stories between 29 and 26 yawned off to his right. Rogers breathed out and moved on down to the second step.

The average human adult has 5 liters of blood, you've got plenty more.

The second step gave way, and Rogers fell, arms pinwheeling and searching for a grip. He cursed his luck and tumbled down the government built metal stairs. His knees buckled and pain flowed through his limbs. He saw the next level coming up to meet him amid a tangle of arms and fingers.

Before he passed out, the last thing he saw was the number 28 floating in front of him like an apparition, spinning out and disappearing into the dust. He heard more creaking, and then, silence.

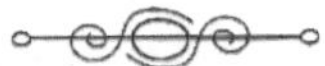

When Rogers awoke, he was surrounded by demons. 241 was gone, replaced by a hellish landscape of endless night. The creatures were half human and half some sort of wolfish creature, like a dingo only with a longer nose.

Foul black spittle dripped from their scarred and decayed lips and unnatural tongues produced more copiously. Their eyes were black as the night from which they came. Rogers was up and running as fast as his legs would allow, strangely sluggish compared to the world he was in. Lightning crashed around him in a landscape devoid of detail, lighting it up like strobe flashes at a nightclub.

The wolf-things howled and the night only grew colder around him. He ran, movements casting jerky shadows due to the perpetual lightning. He could see a building up ahead, its facade illuminated briefly amongst the lightning.

It was a church. Decrepit and unused, Rogers didn't think twice before running in to hide. If he had looked, he would have noticed that there was not a single cross on the building. There was, however, a symbol, the crest of the government, a dragon with crossed swords.

The door gave easily as he shouldered through into its dusty hallways.

The floor was littered with corpses. They were mostly human. Actually, they were all human, but altered into grotesque shapes by their untold suffering. There was the corpse of a woman, emaciated and in the advanced stages of decomposition, who died at the window, arms outstretched as if welcoming the morning sun.

The detective struggled to contain his sanity. Outside the wolf things howled once more.

He took a deep breath, and started making his way past the corpses, hesitant to disturb the bodies, still wrought with agony in the way that they lay on the floor. He had seen pictures of mass graves, but nothing like this. He could feel the utter desperation and fear these people had felt, and struggled to clamp down on his rising sense of panic.

He heard a voice;

Amazing Grace, so sweet the sound

The hellscape brightened, like the lifting of a storm. The wolf-things snarled once more.

And he awoke again.

241 swam back into vision, the gray walls and Government Issue décor coming back by degrees. Rogers groaned and rolled over, struggling to get up. Pain, formerly dulled and throbbing, now spiked in agony throughout his leg again. He really needed to find a medkit, fast and soon. He could also feel a bruise forming where he'd landed on his holster, adding to the general pain all over his body.

As kneeled on one leg, a folder caught his eye. Balancing it on his good knee, he opened the folder, leaving bloodstains on the edges. The report was some kind of medical report, all graphs and numbers. He searched for a passage or an intro, some clue.

> *Subject 171*
> *This appears to be our most promising subject. We knew that the infusion of nanites could always bring unexpected side effects in those deemed especially intuitive or good but he's either having full blown hallucinations or has actively breached the quantum barrier.*
> *Studies show that nanites increase cortical activity in response to stress.*
> *It seems that we are clear to proceed to the next stage with this patient.*

The rest was all test scores and procedures, so he threw the report aside. Rogers gingerly tried to walk on his leg, the spike of pain that still shot up dissuaded him from trying that again. He'd seen some grim government testing facilities in his time, mostly on criminals or indentured subjects, but none of this made sense as to why he'd been sent here.

He looked around and saw that he'd landed in what appeared to be the processing level of the facility, rooms for interviews and benches for tests lined up around the place. The sign on the wall said LEVEL -26- PRIMARY TESTING.

Shit, Rogers looked up at the frayed stairwell, now framed by the light coming in from the skylight/entrance… 3 levels up. He supposed he was lucky to be breathing. But he could have sworn he'd fallen only one level. Shining the flashlight on the now broken stairs he could see that the section of stairway had given way and fallen on another weak section, thus causing him to fall further. He was lucky, indeed.

Some luck I have…

There, by the wall, was the basic first aid kit, government issue looking strangely out of place amidst all the desks and empty chairs. Rogers didn't care what it was there for, he shambled on over there and tore the door open, searching for bandages, anything that would help.

In one of the shelves, he found a local antiseptic and a series of bandages. Using scissors to cut away the fabric, he poured a bit onto the wound. Pain, not as bad as before spiked through his legs.

He heard a scream.

Dropping the bottle, Rogers whipped around, looking for something, anything. Only the sound of the bottle as it rolled away remained to answer him.

Probably all this blood loss…

Rogers reassessed his priorities, he had to find a way out of here before any more sentries or anti-intruder devices did him any more damage, or worse, killed him. The case was gone to shit anyway, no one mentioned med bays and labs and government traps. The stairway was out, unless he could find a ladder in this fucking place.

He moved along the hallways, flashlight bobbing all over the place. Only now that he was three levels deep inside an abandoned government facility did he truly realized the stupidity that led him to this situation.

Maybe I should retire...

There up ahead, Rogers spotted an elevator, a way out. Still limping, but now limping with a purpose, he made his way through the processing area, passed all the loose pieces of reports and scripts scattered about like confetti. His flashlight splayed over scattered stationery and dusty keyboards casting shadows over empty chairs, abandoned in haste. Rogers had no doubt whatever happened here, happened too quickly for people to pick up their things. But all the usual markers, things like fire, explosion, and leaks usually left some sort of sign.

He approached the elevator, the steel doors were closed firmly shut, and he didn't want to try to pry them open in his current state. The button was probably unpowered, but Rogers tried anyway.

The panel likewise bore no fruit. Rogers knew that eventually someone would come for him, but he knew they'd get here too late. He resolved to searching the desks of the processing area for anything that could help him signal for help.

The first desk he tried was full of your usual office crap, stationery, a picture of someone's daughter, memos about reports. On a hunch, he tried the power for one of the consoles. Nothing.

Frustrated, he cast his flashlight around hurriedly in the darkened space, feeling utterly defeated.

Something clanged across the room. Roger's flashlight was up, and now that his other hand was not trying to stem his blood loss anymore, it was halfway reaching for his sidearm.

His flashlight found nothing. He resumed his search.

Eventually, he found a fuse box, and managed to get the lights working. The processing area brightened, and he could see interview rooms and benches, hopefully with their own medical supplies. Rogers was no medic, but he sure could use some basic supplies.

As he moved amongst the desks, he noticed some of the monitors were online. Pausing at one, he saw that they had emails open;

To: PROCCESSING   STAFF
(staff@gmsc241.gov)
From: RESEARCH
(research@gmsc241.gov)
Please note that staff are not to share
food with participants under any

conditions whatsoever. The scientists need their subjects to be as uncontaminated as possible once they enter the facility.
Thank you for your co-operation

And another, more personal note;

From: ldragon (#1254@gmsc241.gov)
To: Leela (l.muranga@gmsc241.gov)
Hey there beautiful,
Got some time for a quick lunch?
Meet me in the storeroom, and don't bring any food.
Xoxo your little dragon "teeheee"

Rogers looked around for any more useful supplies, starting with the storeroom. There were no signs of the illicit meeting that took place here, nothing but dusty crates of medicinal supplies. Something nagged at him, but he knew he couldn't stay. Trying his luck again at the elevator, he tried the button again and to his relief it worked. He pressed the button, and somewhere within the rest of the facility he could hear wheels turning and locks clanking. The elevator made a reassuring noise as it made its way up through the levels, one by one. Rogers stared at the counter; it was at level 15 and climbing.

He decided to look around a bit more whilst he waited, at another monitor, another email caught his eye.

FROM: Andrew Petersen, Research Team Lead (A.Petersen@gmsc241.gov)
TO: Amanda Rosen, Processing Team Leader (A.Rosen@gmsc241.gov)

Subject 172
Please retire subject 172, she is of low potential. I understand that she may actually be a security risk as she has powerful relatives, which the capture team failed to account for. Take care of it, please, quietly. She may have gotten a glimpse of Subject 171 down on level 1. Before you reply with an angry email, Yes, I know Capture fucked up, but what can we do? She's here now and has seen a bunch of things she shouldn't have. I don't want to go up before the review board and explain a leak. Better this is handled in house, if you catch my drift.
A. Petersen
Research Team Leader

This Amanda person didn't take kindly to that, in the next email she wrote;

Petersen,

If we terminate her, we'll have breached protocol. If we create any sort of statistically significant anomaly, the rest of the world will know. That's why we recruit so widely geographically, a little bit here and a little bit there.
Are you sure indoctrination and alteration can't be done?

The elevator pinged and Rogers looked inside, flashlight out in case it wasn't lit. It was empty, he got in and pressed no.1. As the Elevator rose, he tried to tie the various threads together. This was no ordinary government research facility, and the signs here didn't point to it simply being abandoned. He was starting to put together a plan of coming back with proper tools when he heard the wolves begin to howl.

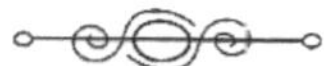

The faithful continued to watch their goddess's dreams. She writhed and screamed and the screen showed images of her nightmares. The wolf-things were snarling, and pictures of the dead and dying flashed by one by one.

The faithful knew that this was par for the course, and yet they waited. They were rewarded for their patience with images of a building. As these images were displayed, the goddess strained against her restraints and almost tore the cables out of her skin. Some members of her congregation wiped the spittle from her mouth, and readjusted the cables. The rest watched on in silence.

The next image was of one single man in an elevator, all alone.

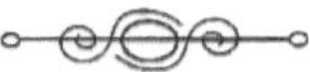

The elevator was losing power. Somewhere between 26 and 28 the light started flickering and the car started to slow down. Rogers had hoped he'd have a ticket at least up to 29 so that he could get up the same way he came in, but he doubted he'd be able to get out of this elevator if it got stuck. He cursed his lack of backup yet again.

The elevator came to a jarring halt. Above, he heard something snap. Rogers held his breath.

The elevator came loose, and fell. Rogers was battered about the cabin. He could hear the emergency brakes screaming but a lack of maintenance meant that they would fail.

What a way to go...

Strangely, he still heard that bone chilling sound, overcoming the fear of his imminent death in the elevator. The numbers on the panel flashed by 23, 22, 21.

"Why are you here?"

He started at the sound of that voice. There was a young girl in the elevator with him.

"You're not real." He said, almost yelling over the screaming brakes.

"Tell me why you're here." The numbers kept ticking by even faster 15, 14, 13, and he heard a *clunk* and the screaming stopped, and the elevator fell faster.

Ah, what the fuck...

"I'm looking for a boy."

"Why?"

"Because it's my job."

The numbers kept ticking; Rogers stared at the panel, waiting for his inevitable death.

"Are you going to hurt him?" The girls stare bored into his, she was unperturbed by

"What? No, I just want to find him. Please."

The elevator stopped.

Rogers stared at the girl. Who was she? Why did she look vaguely familiar?

She floated out the doors into the darkness. Her body emitted a glow. Rogers was never a superstitious man. He'd seen and heard things that lesser minded folk would consider near miraculous. But still, the girl emitted an angelic glow.

He followed her awestruck, climbing gingerly out of the elevator.

"How did you make the elevator stop?"

She didn't answer him. She chose instead to float onwards through the corridor. Rogers looked around, and saw the painted 1 that meant he was in the bottom of the facility.

The very heart of the facility didn't have a name, it was simply labeled "Link Research".

The girl disappeared through a doorway up ahead. Roger ran or hobbled after her.

"Wait, Who are you? And what is this place?" He asked.

"Come, and you will see", she said, gesturing to a monitor.

The rest of the facility was dark, and yet, this monitor was powered.

> *Research report #1*
> *LEVEL BLACK*
> *Nanotechnology gave humanity many gifts. Health, sense, repairs, connection, it changed human physiology in ways and forms that scientists and politicians could never have anticipated. The glittering silver genie, once let out of the bottle could not be contained.*
> *By inducing nanotechnology into subjects in controlled doses, we can see exponentially what benefits this technology can bring.*

Rogers scrolled down; most of it was about the benefits and structure of nano-machines.

Research Report#34
LEVEL BLACK
We've successfully aerosolized a variant of the nanites. Potentials are now exposed in it when they go through processing. Needless to say, our own staff must be quarantined to prevent exposure.

So that's what they were doing down here, experimenting on people, invasive procedures. He turned to the girl, who had been watching him intensely.

He said, "This still doesn't answer my questions."

She still stared at him, expressionless; "Come".

She led him into another room, this time with a corpse. Rogers stared at the corpse it was literally the only body he'd seen in this facility. Given how weird the situation was, he expected it to be his client.

But no, it was a full-fledged adult, but as he gingerly turned it over, he saw the face and stood back in shock. He was too experienced around bodies to show any disgust, but the face.

The face was that of the wolf-things. The elongated nose, the teeth, the skin.

Back around the bowels of level 1, the wolf-things howled once more.

Her mouth was open in a silent scream, as her voice had given out hours ago. Her face contorted in an expression of utmost terror, and the monitor continued flashing images. The faithful were starting to get worried, murmurs of concern and prayers of health being muttered. Most had averted their eyes, except those closest who watched on in dreadful fascination. Her movements had become frantic yet tired, as if whatever torment she was in had somehow grown worse but she was fast running out of energy.

Some of the workers thought they should forcibly disconnect their oracle from the machine. But they didn't know if it would make the visions stop.

Time and time again, the clearest image jumbled amongst the kaleidoscope of dreams was of that man, that man with a flashlight, and a gun.

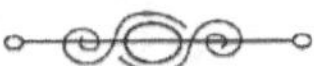

He had three rounds left. After seeing one of those wolf things alive, he was taking no chances. After the first howl, the girl or rather, the apparition had disappeared just as mysteriously as she had appeared. Rogers backed out and tried to get to the elevator.

He had heard footsteps that were strange, like a halfway shuffle between a walk and a run, or his limp. He pulled his firearm in one swift motion and aimed it down the hallway.

Nothing.

Nothing but the sound of his own breathing.

He turned back to the elevator.

He heard a fast thudding, like a run. Rogers turned around and fired without thinking. The gun went off like god's thunder, and a black shape hit the ground at his feet.

17, 16, 15. Three rounds, no hits.

It was one of those wolf things; the teeth, the eyes.

It was still alive, growling at Gryn. He put another round in his head, his hands shaking from the adrenaline.

Rogers waited, and listened. Nothing else came through but the sound of his heart.

"You must hurry!" Rogers started and almost shot the wall where the girl appeared.

"I don't know how I'm supposed to get out of here."

The girl went up against the elevator panel and placed her palm on the button. As if by magic, the panel lit up and light began to come back to this level.

"Go now. Gryn, and tell the world of what you've seen."

"But what about the boy?"

"He isn't here, now go!"

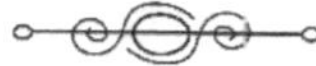

The sun had set over the city, and the lights of its residents provided an unnatural glow. The workday had ended, and people were going home. In the shrine the girl stopped writhing, the worshippers murmur died down. The monitor was silent.

The worshippers started leaving, one by one, until save for her most dedicated caretakers, there was no one left in the shrine.

A trench coated man with his collar turned up walked in surreptitiously, but he was observed. A caretaker came up to him and said, "The visions have stopped for today, please, come back later."

Rogers turned to the caretaker, a frail old man, and said to him. "I know who she is."

Leaning down beside the insensate girl, he whispered, "Thank you," and left something in her hand, curling her fingers around it.

The caretaker slowly uncurled the girl's fingers and found a photograph.

The photograph was of the daughter, from the stationery cabinet in a long forgotten government facility, and on the back was written;

I'll find him, for you.
-Gryn.

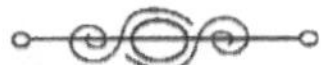

Concept idea given to authors to write story = A pious detective who has the ability to walk between worlds is trapped within a deserted government building. He must find (something) that will vindicate/redeem his client and/or himself.

Moyukh Muzahid is officially a student of law and journalism at Murdoch. Unofficially, he's a massive reader and sometimes writer of science fiction. He loves the post-apocalypse, and enjoys a good video game or 10. Having lived in Singapore and Sydney, he now calls Perth home. He is new to the writing game, but hopes to write his first novel soon.

One's True Self

BY **D.C. DAINES**

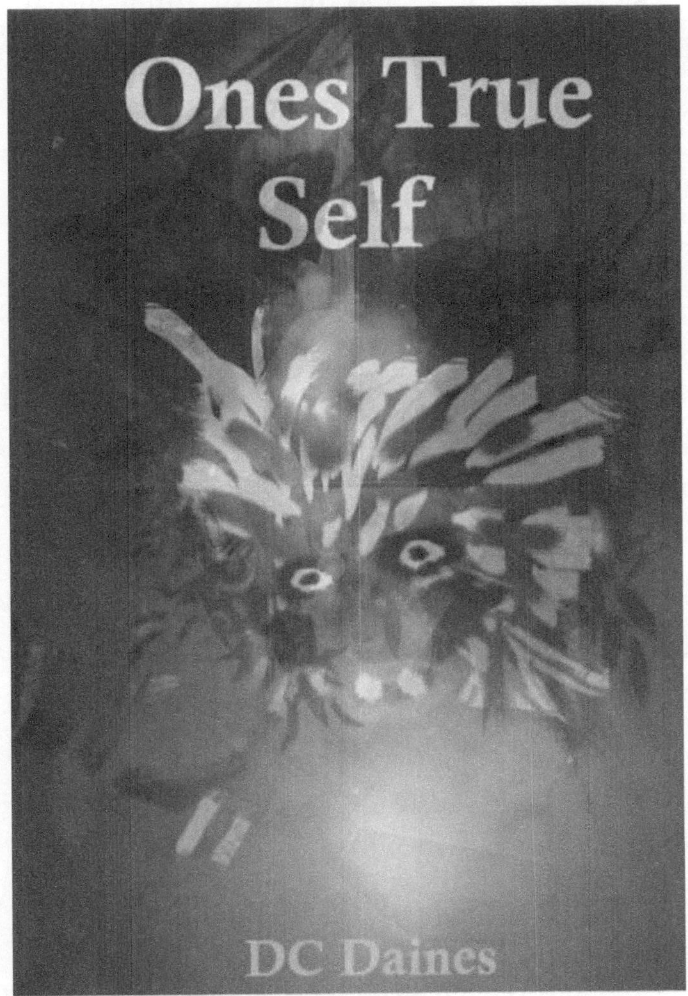

"Nah man, I don't want to do it." What did I have to say to convince her?

"You need to see."

"Seriously, I don't. If anything bad can happen man, it will happen to me." I knew it could and I knew it would. You know, one of those guys that everything and anything will happen to? Well that is me.

"You need to see, my love. See what I see. Feel what I feel." Her hand stroked my shoulder, my neck, my arm and as a shiver rolled down my back I pulled away from her inviting caress.

"No seriously, it is not an option. What the Fuck man, I said..." Something was wrong! The pain was intense, originating from my MHU, building until it was shooting up my arm, burning my blood. No way, not this way, not now, not like this. "What did..." the pain took over me, my body shaking, my mind screaming for it to end, and then whatever had entered my blood stream collided with even that. The black tunnel conceived by my failing brain did nothing to calm me as I neared its end. Devouring me, her stunning blood-shot and glazed eyes look into mine, "you dr..." She stopped the accusation with a gentle finger upon my lips, a claw? Her voice lowered as she stroked my hair, whispering through clenched teeth... fangs?

"You will see what I see, you will feel what I feel, you will be one with me, and then you will see, I am not insane.

They are real! We are real. We are forever. We are unique. You are mine for all time!" and then she was gone, the halo around her swallowed by the darkness.

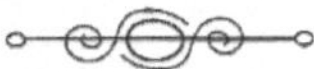

"Insert health stimulant... Health levels critical. Manually insert health stimulant." The metallic voice originating from my burning forearm woke me, but it did nothing for my nerves or my heart rate as it continued to climb. Flicking my arm around I tried to focus on the sound. Finding it, I think, I fumbled with the controls, however my numb hands could not quite push the right sequence. My eyes tried to guess at which of the two controls and appendages before me actually existed. Sparks flew from the MHU's attached to my arm. Not a normal occurrence and almost as painful as the trauma I had experienced before losing consciousness. Oh, yeah, you would not know what a MHU was. Imagine a computer on your arm, a personal assistant, wired into your body functions, telling you when to eat, drink, and take a crap. Well that would be last year's version of the *Medical Help Unit.* The new one tells you when to ask a girl out, when to go to sleep, how much to eat, when you are lying, when someone else is lying and so on. It leaves nothing to chance, nothing to the imagination and definitely will not allow you to do something illegal. So then what just happened?

My torn and dirty jacket absorbed the tears as I wiped them from my eyes, making it easier to see the small cracked screen and the buttons upon it; the green one for pain, yellow for mental anguish and the red for serious injury. Now which one should I choose? I certainly couldn't input any command codes, this was the next best thing. The flashing touch screen sizzled again; this was not good. I had never known of one of these devices being damaged before. Malfunction, yes. That is why they had the manual controls, for the interim measures until a MHU task force could get to you. Pain forced its way through my whole body again, searing through me as my back arched, my muscles cramping. Following the forward motion of my body as they relaxed, I slumped, hitting a button. Don't ask me which color, but the relief was instant. The mind-blowing drums beating within my skull started to subside, now combining with the lesser burning sensation, my body becoming a dull throb.

Where is she? There was nothing to give me a clue... or was there? A rusty tin bin was beside me, lid half hanging off, its contents of wood and cardboard spilling out. A concrete wall that had seen better days behind me, quite uncomfortable too as the broken rubble from a gaping hole dug into my back. The coldness through my jeans was only amplified by the steel of the floor and the damp that had collected overnight. My hand combed through my hair, wet, but no blood as it stuck to my scalp.

My blurred eyes searched further through the dim light, sunrise yet to poke out its head. Glasses, oh I forgot my glasses. Fumbling, I searched around me for them, only to find that they had taken up residence in my upper pocket. Their small wire frame was cold against my skin as I placed them upon my pointy nose.

Nothing; no sign of her. What had she done to me? What had she done with herself? She had been talking weird for days. Saying that she had something that she needed to tell me; that she was unusual, unique, uncommon, and dangerous; and I was her soul-mate, the one and only true form of her eternal love. Her soul-mate. Wow, if this is what happens when you take a girl's flower, I am pretty sure I never want to do that again. Saying that, she only started acting funny after taking... something caught my attention, with my nose raised I started to sniff, the hint of stale body odor in the air. A feeling of dread opened within me, from where I did not know, the hairs upon the back of my neck standing to attention, my pain, all but forgotten as I felt around behind me.

"Ha, you mine boy. Give me ya clothes." He stank of a mixture of liquor, stale sweat and vomit, the stench assaulting my nostrils as he ambled towards me to grab me by the collar of my jacket. His face so close to mine, his breathe in my mouth. Turning I expelled what little that had resided in my stomach. "Ya punk." Pain followed as his backhand collided with my cheekbone, blood spilling to the ground below. "Ya will lick that off ma boot." My face planted on the boot, its worn leather tearing at my mouth as he forced me down. With all my effort I pushed my body up and tried to break his grip, but to no avail as I was filled with panic. Yet, his skull felt unusually malleable under the force of the metal rod as I brought it from behind the tin bin and across his head. Thump. His body sinking to the ground as his grip and mine released, the metal rod clanging to the floor as I jumped up and ran.

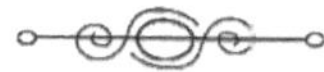

"Officer, yes, my son is missing." The voice held an edge of desperation that showed on the face of the woman in the video monitor as she continued to answer the questions being fired at her in quick succession.

"No, he does not normally do this! He has never done this before."

"Yes he is always home before curfew."

"I have already tried his girlfriends."

"No I do not think they are off doing the *Nasty*."

"Can you take me seriously, I am his mother?"

"He has been gone all night."

"Yes officer, our last name is Ware."

"His girlfriend's last name is Wolf."

"No, I am not kidding."

"He is sixteen in a week."

"No he has not shown any signs of changing. He is a good boy. What is this about?"

"No he has never taken off his MHU, however I am not sure if it is functional as I cannot locate him."

"Her parents are worried too as she has not returned home either and her MHU is also off-line."

"Yes. That is what I said. I believe this is serious. That is why I called you."

"Yes I will be home."

"Thank you Officer."

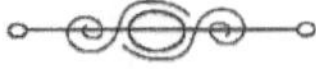

Vomit; sick; throw up. However you say it, I had spent the better part of ten minutes doing it and I stank. I am not sure if it was the extreme distance I had just covered as I sprinted full out and away from death. Or if it was the knowledge that I had just injured somebody, and badly, if not killed them. I continued dry retching.

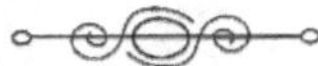

The young officer stood proud in front of the screen, his uniform pressed to perfection, his tie a bright blue, his uniform a deep red. The screen before him was a deep black. His hands fidgeted behind him as he spoke, the slight hint of apprehension in his voice as he was now on the receiving end of quick and angry questions.

"Commander, I believe we have a situation."

"Yes Sir, I am sorry. I know you were asleep. However this is important."

"Yes I want to keep my job."

"No I do not know how much a street cleaner makes."

"No Sir, I do not want to find out."

"Excuse me Sir, but you really need to hear me out."

"Yes Sir, I know who I am talking to."

"No Sir, I am not being facetious."

"But Sir, we may have a—"

"A—"

"Sir, if you stop ranting at me, I can explain."

"We may have another changing happening—"

"Yes Sir, I should have said that straight away."

"Yes Sir, I know how important this is."

"Yes Sir, I will get onto it."

"That is Command code Contain Alpha 1?"

"The Tracker, Sir?"

"Yes Sir, I can hear you."

"All right Sir, The Tracker it is."

"And the families?"

"Yes Sir, there are two."

"No Sir, I am sorry. I should have mentioned that earlier, Sir."

"Yes Sir, I understand."

"The families can never know Sir."

"Yes Sir, you will deal with it, thank you Sir."

Click.

"This is Officer Sun. I have just spoken to the Commander. I have been given authorization to wake The Tracker. Command code Contain Alpha 1."

"I understand what that means."

"Yes, I will take full responsibility."

"I will be there momentarily."

"Yes I will bring the choker."

Click.

The voice demanded attention as it projected out of the black screen, a hint of tiredness creeping in as the Commander repeated his prior sentence. "Code verification. Military Commander Garret, 12893TSD."

"Activate *The Small Dragon.*"

"Send message to Global... Mr. Haynes, we have an issue. It seems that the cover story needs to be put into play. We need an extraction team and removal. It would be appreciated if this were kept out of the books and away from the prying eyes of our superiors. And yes, you told me so. I will buy you that drink next time you are on Alpha base. Oh, and Simon. This conversation never happened. Commander Anthony Ferret Garret out."

Click.

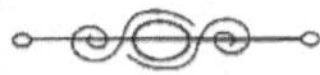

Stumbling forward I grabbed for something, anything to keep me up, nothing came into reach as I fell onto my hands. The stance seeming surprisingly natural as I lowered into it, my shoulders high, my behind low in a crouch and my nose raised to the sky. The stench of my expelled insides almost overpowered all else. Almost! I could smell her, she was on heat and I knew it. On heat? Her aroma aroused me, her scent irresistible as I started to bound down the alley. The area around me disappeared quickly, my agility getting more insane at each corner. Scaling bins or anything else in my way with one leap, until finally I stopped. My nose to the air, I knew this was the place. Up, I needed to go up, to be jumping from balcony to balcony as I made haste towards her.

Straightening, I corrected myself into a human like stance, the MHU flashing as it insisted I inject myself further with a painkiller of sorts. The sparks did nothing but stimulate me further now, the pain a pleasant side-effect of its malfunctioning. The screen flashed, message. I could see it was from Mother. Mother. Now why would she be calling me? No matter, there was a nagging pull of my attention back to the door as I caught my girlfriend's scent again. That readiness to be taken, and I was eager to take her. The door crumbled easily under my force; well it would have if I had wanted it to, their throats hanging from their torn necks. I corrected these thoughts just in time, knocking on the door. The commotion inside explained to me that they were expecting no one. Well that is what one of them said, whilst the other told him to get her into the bedroom and not to come out until he was called. I could hear the rifle being cocked, the drugs being shuffled into the square table in the lounge room, the needles clicking together as they were thrown in in haste.

"Why are we hiding? We just want the money her and her boyfriend owe us after they went postal."

"You forget we killed that little prick after he put our stuff all over the place. He acted like some kind of animal. Went fuckin wild man."

Man, that was my line. Don't man. No man. Stop man. I told them/her not to inject me. Fuckin assholes. My blood boiled as I clenched my fists, blood dripping from my palms as my claws dug in. My eyes burnt again as I stared down the door, wanting to rip it from its hinges once again. One of their hearts beat faster as I heard him dragging someone into another room; their mass thrown onto the bed and his heart beat faster again.

"Don't even think of it man, or I'll kill you myself." Sounds of another shotgun cocking was all I needed to spring into action, the door still closed.

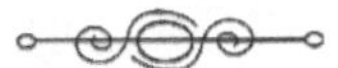

"What the fuck man, there is no one here!?" As he poked his head of scruffy hair and week old facial fluff out the doorway, the man peered out through his bloodshot eyes. The shotgun was pointed at the ceiling as he scuffed further into the hallway, his head sweeping from side to side with the shotgun following. The gunshot screamed through the air, replaced by plaster dust from the ceiling and the crack of the man's arm as it was snapped. It hung there useless, broken in two, no longer allowing him to lift his finger to the trigger. A forced, one-handed cock of the shotgun resonated through the rooms and then gurgling. His eyes bulged, the gun falling to the floor where his feet had been seconds earlier. The hand that grasped his throat tightened as his eyes screamed for the mercy he no longer could. His larynx gone, shattered by the force, feet flailing and looking for a perch. The growl was low, quiet and controlled, but the power it resonated was unmissable. With one last clench from the hairy hand around the neck, it snapped and the hallway became alight in sparks.

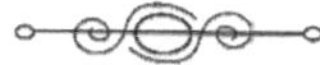

I could hear the guy's heart beating faster as he came out of the doorway, the shotgun cocked and ready to shoot anyone without question, including me. The thrill of it stimulated me as I came up behind him, the excitement driving my heart faster. My senses heightened, I could see the sweat upon his neck, dripping over the goose bumps as he shuffled from the room. One thing on his mind, sheer terror, kill or be killed. I knew this was going to be my only chance; my one option to get my girlfriend, my Amy, out. The power coursed through me, my nails growing in length and sharpness and I knew what I had to do. The thick hair tickled as it followed, pushing through

272

my skin where fine hair had been moments earlier. I marveled at my hand, following the growth further to the MHU on my arm. A gunshot startled me, tearing me from my own trance. I turned to the threat; the dust from the ceiling concealed everything before me. My MHU sparked and I was gone, inside the room, the door slamming. The bolts locked in place and then I was before the bedroom door. I could hear the filthy breathing of the other man upon her. Breathing into her ear, whispering what he would like to do with her as he rubbed himself up her bare leg. He had not even the sense to heed the warning of the gunshot in the corridor. The loyalty to come to his friends, no friend is too strong a word, his acquaintances aid. I could sense her heart beat quickening, feel her anxiousness at what was about to happen. He screamed, his drug-ridden body screamed. Screamed for peace, for a reprieve from the disgust he put into it, day after day. But the scream was not for that. It was for the sight before him. As he had tried to rip her blouse from her chest, I had broken down the door. His arms that were bolstered to tear her clothes from her were in the air. His feet also flailing as I slammed his back to the floor and his breath left him. She was upon him, her fangs bared, her eyes blood red as she broke her restraints and took to him. Pinning both his arms to the floor, her nails tearing at his wrists.

Mmm, something I had not noticed before. He did not have a MHU. For that matter, neither did the guy in the corridor. So why did they not have them? Was it because they were drug dealers? Pondering on this idea was not an option as Amy, or the creature before me in Amy's body, went for the throat of the guy on the floor. My backhand collided with her face, her fangs biting deep in my flesh, and yet it felt natural, almost playful, as though I needed to enforce my dominance. Her body went backwards, her clawed hands hitting the ground first, her arms lowered her body as it flipped backwards, just enough to let her spring onto the bed on all fours as she growled at me. With shoulders lowered I dropped my stance, circling the outskirts of the bed as I made my way to her. Claws raked at me, snarls told me to beware, but her eyes and scent told me to take her. What was I doing? What was I becoming? What did I care? I just wanted her and she wanted me, that is all that mattered. Cliiiiiiiiiick, the trigger was pulled as though in slow motion. I could sense it over the other stimulations now crowding my mind. My body reacted, spinning around to the sound, my mind with no time to respond, purely primal. The barrel felt hot against my hand as I angled it away from my chest, the force spinning the man around as the pellets splattered across the room. I could feel flesh tearing from my shoulder, the pellets burning through my flesh, taking with it splatters of blood.

"We, we, we, k-killed yo-ou." He screamed as the shotgun was sent across the room; a look of desperation and disbelief across his face.

"You what?" It did not make sense till now. The guy they said they killed, it was me. They killed me? They killed me? Well I was not about to let it happen again. But if I was dead, how was I alive? Was this a dream? He took advantage of my hesitation, my confusion, a knife seemed to appear from nowhere and he flew at me, only a few feet, but it was enough time for me to react. The knife fell to the floor, his hand no longer able to grip it. Or was it his wrist no longer supported it as it lay sliced open? Never mind, his hand was almost severed to the bone and the knife no longer posed a threat. Warmness filled me as the blood pulsed from the arm he was now clutching, every beat matching his heart as he tried to put himself back together. Hunger, I felt hunger. I needed to eat.

My throat constricted, chest puffed out and I spoke, no, I growled at him in a slow and methodical manner as I raised my shoulders in question. "Man, you killed me?" His eyes just kept jumping around me, the blood still spurting as he tried to mouth something. Something was wrong; I could feel it. Another presence; someone or something stalking me. Neck hairs raised again, a deep throated growl came from me and as I could hear the front door shatter to a million pieces, I watched as the man before me was thrust into the air, a clawed hand exploding from his chest. Amy was on my shoulder, I am not sure how, she was just there. My body fleeing from the window, the ledge, the fire escape and finally onto the ground. I did not stop to see whether the howls were from a creature hunting me, or if it was still following me. I did not turn to see where the sparks were originating from, or the flashes of light that filled the alley as though in time with the howls. I just fled.

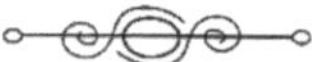

"Mum, we are in trouble. She is bleeding badly. I did not know where else to go. Mum!" I could hear my voice screaming, the door wide open; my mother standing in the doorway as though to stop me from entering. My voice pleaded, my eyes tearing in time with hers, but no voice came out of her mouth. She just kept voicing the same thing. What was it? What was she trying to say? I could not... oh fuck. Leaning forward I sniffed the air, trying to get past the smell of our own blood now plastered across our clothing; the hairs on the back of my neck once again bristling up. Shudders rolled down my spine. Shadows proved what I had just scented. There were others inside; ones that were not part of my family, not part of Amy's. They were there, mind you, Amy's family, yet the others smelt different. Sterile, like they were told what to wear, their scents all the same, the same gel in their hair. I wouldn't doubt it if they had on the same clothes. Either way, their scent was pungent to my nose. Listening closely I could hear them.

"Wait till he is inside. We want them to come peacefully..." The clip clopping of business shoes resonated through the hall as he walked from the foyer and into the lounge, leaving the others where they were, quiet and waiting in the shadows. Then he started preaching with a matter of fact tone, the other people in the room he had entered were silent, gulping from time to time as the voice paused for affect. "Mr. Ware, Mr. Wolf, you have to believe us, this drug is unpredictable. The kids that take it are unpredictable... your kids... it is a new synthetic that has been peddled by pushers to allow them to bypass the MHU and ultimately render the MHU useless. It is called The Small Dragon, as it has the effect of turning those that take it into uncontrollable animals. They feel as though they are different, that they have a purpose, bigger than anyone else, and they have no remorse. If you get in their way, they will kill you, family or not. We just need you to co-operate for a little while longer and we will get your children back safely, without any more loss of life... however, due to the lives they have taken, you know they must be exiled?" Exiled, what was she talking about? Lives we took, they can't have found out about that already, it had only been minutes, hadn't it?

Mother's eyes pleaded with me once more as she caught my attention once again. "Run, get out of here, don't come back." These were the words she wanted me to hear, she did not have to repeat herself yet again. I was gone. I could hear the turmoil in the house, my mother's screams as she was pushed to the ground, her bones breaking as the men trampled her and the bullets as they flew past my head, but I kept going. Zigzagging, jumping, leaping, Amy's weight upon my shoulder barely registering on my adrenaline filled body. Selfish or not, I had to, that is what my mother had wanted, what she had sacrificed for, another bone cracked as the head of the group came running out, his thick shoes breaking her fingers as he walked upon her.

"I know you can hear me boy," he whispered upon the wind, crushing mother's fingers further. "If you want to see your family again, you will come peacefully, you will surrender and you will die like the animal you have become." And then I was too far away to hear, to hear my mother crying; my father's screams at the abuse of her before he was knocked to the floor with the butt of a rifle; the tears from Amy's parents as they raced to the door and watched their little girl being carried away.

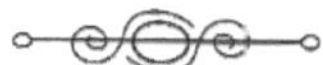

"Honey? Honey? Honey?" Her voice rose in pitch with each call, her heart beat quicker at each breath and I was glad. She was conscious and alive and that is all that mattered. But, I had no idea what to do now. Somehow our wounds had healed overnight. I was unaware of how long it had been, or even how long I had run. I remembered dropping to the ground in an exhausted mess, laying Amy's body upon my bloodied jacket and passing out. And now, we were awake. For five minutes I had been observing, checking our wounds, our surroundings, and making sure we were safe. Dried blood caked our clothes, our flesh and our hair, yet we had no wounds. Scars, yes. It seemed that advanced healing had its disadvantages, the skin did not heal properly, scars in each area I had taken a wound, and there were a lot. I stepped over the spent bullets that had made their way out of my flesh and onto the cold floor, and reached out to grasp her hand. She rose from the ground, her breath warm in my ear as she hugged me, her scent stimulated me, her warmth aroused me as our lips met, clothes torn from our bodies as we grasped each other, growling in passion. My teeth bit down on her lip, drawing blood which I savored, the taste salty, sweet and wonderful. Her body reacted to mine as she rubbed herself upon my leg. I ran a claw down her chest, her bosom open and beckoning me as I lowered her to the pile of rags now strewn upon the floor. Our hearts beat as one; our eyes alight with lust, hunger and power as I thrust myself into her howling flesh.

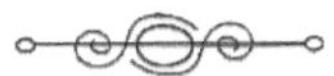

"Run. Run. Run." These were the only words I could muster as my breath left me again and I leapt from another ledge, the wind leaving me as I smacked into the corresponding fire escape. We needed to escape and we had no idea where we were going. Amy was right behind me but she did not have the power I possessed, she was sleeker, she was... Well she was my reason for living, for running, for fighting. Explaining it seems futile, I just knew it, without her, my existence would be over. My breath returned, not a minute too soon as she landed beside me, her eyes alight with the fire I had never known her to possess.

My open claw slashed out, the beast bounding the same path we had just traversed altered his course mid-air as though he controlled it, missing my deadly swipe and slamming into the ladder beside me. Its restraints shattered instantly, starting its drop to three stories below, the monster's grasp still on its rungs. He was a majestic beast, I could appreciate, yet this was not the time. As the ladder fell he was already bounding up its rungs to our safe haven. Grasping her arm I pulled at Amy. She needed no further prompting as we leapt again, the metal grating shuddering and echoing down the dark streets at our force. As he gained again I knew I had no hope. He was far superior, stronger, larger, more powerful, more skilled, and I am being under complimentary. He was the perfect predator, and I had to protect Amy. I could only see one way out and it did not bode well for me.

Her arm was slender in my grip, her eyes questioning as I caressed her elbow. Our pace was fast, not stopping for the intended embrace and then we were there, my hand wrapped around the pole before me, her weight registering for a second as our momentum sent us spinning around it and then I let her go. Her beauty in her pose as she flew across the expanse left me in awe, my love and need to protect her coming to a crashing end in that moment as the creature's shoulder smashed into my back, my body dropping as my grip was lost, her beauty stolen from my vision. I could hear her land with a clunk. Feel the air change as she turned around in anguish at what I had done and the glare in her eyes, as she knew what was to become of me. The wind exited my lungs as his body crashed upon mine, my ribs cracked and my world exploded in a flash of light.

"No, I want it alive." My blurred eyes tried to make out his image, a red uniform, a blue tie; that smell, like at home. I glimpsed something in his hand. Pain, excruciating pain as the claws raked my back, then more sparks. I could see the man pushing a button; feel the beast above me shake uncontrollably at the electricity now running through his collar. Fighting it, the beast's body dropped to the floor, his claws tearing upon the steel.

"Alive! Tracker. I said alive." He leant down to me, his breath of mint as he spoke to me as though he had no care. "You will track her, you will find her and you will kill her. We cannot have more of your kind loose." He reached down to my neck, patting my head as he continued. "You think you are superior? You are nothing! Just like those of your race that lived on this rock before you, those we tamed." I could feel the collar being placed around my neck; I could not fight the cold steel of it as it burnt into my flesh as he activated it. "And like those before you that did not obey our command, she will be dead along with your unborn litter."

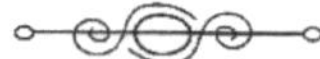

Concept idea given to authors to write story = A child returns to their home to find that nothing/no one is as they left it/them

At 34, D. C. Daines decided that there was more to life than 12 hours at work. Writing is his passion, but his real enjoyment comes from family and friends after they read one of his scenes and he sees their faces light up; they laugh, cry or just call him names, many of which cannot be put in print. More than one of them inspired his imagination and characters in his stories.

With two kids, a boy and a girl, D. C. Daines is looking forward to the good times, the hours of jumping on the trampoline, watching their gymnastics, and being inspired by their little stories and colorful depictions of life. Without his wife being there to tell him to get off the laptop or the gaming console and go to sleep, work, or even eat, he may have become a skeleton in front of the screen...

D.C. Daines is the author of The Star Crystal.

Upon Reflection

BY CONNER KEEGAN

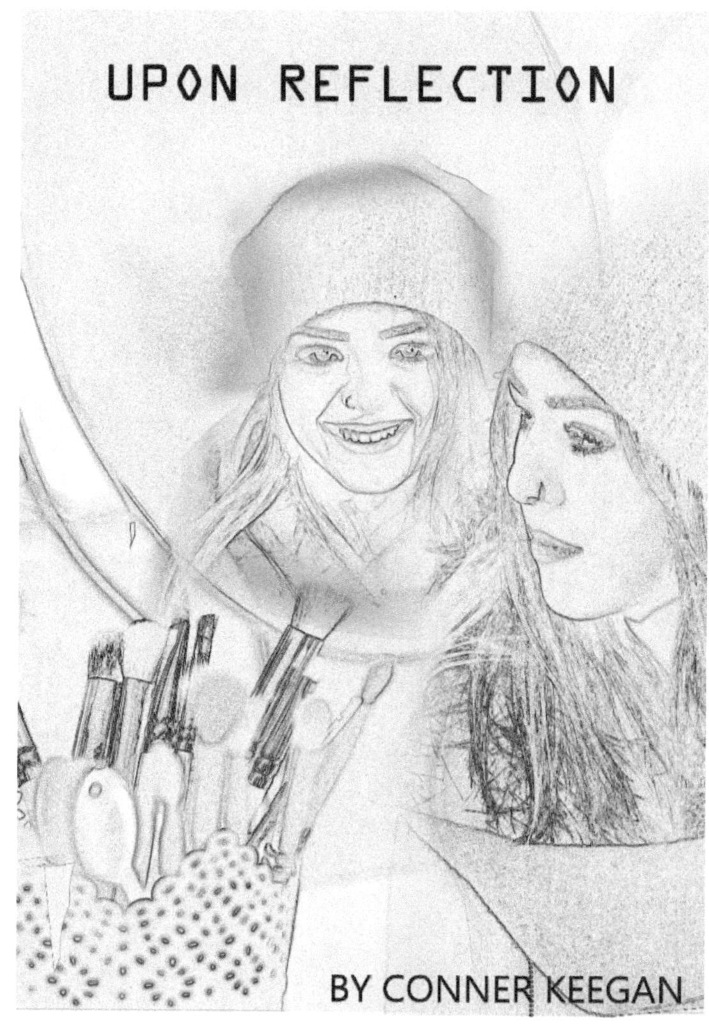

Shantelle stood looking into the mirror. Not as most people would, looking at herself, Shantelle stared into the world on the other side of the mirror, searching for her missing reflection. A plethora of emotions ran through her, fear, sadness, anger. She was very worried.

Seventeen days ago she had stepped through the mirror into this reverse world, while her reflection stepped into hers, as they had done for over a decade. When they had first spoken the spell, that had broken the bond that made them do the same as each other, and they had been trading places for up to two weeks every couple of months ever since.

Shantelle had no idea what to do, or how to communicate with her reflection. If her reflection didn't enter the room in the mirror, she could not contact her. If she moved something around in her room then, the same reflected item would move around in the mirror room. Shantelle was tired and wanted to sleep but did not want to miss her reflection if she came into the room, so she set booby traps around the room to try to wake her if her reflection returned.

She hung a small bell, which she had found in a kitchen drawer tied to a ribbon, around the bedroom door handle.

She opened her closet and threw all of her shoes on the floor so that her reflection would either trip or at least make some noise trying to negotiate a path. She brushed her teeth, took off her clothes and put on the Louvre, Paris t-shirt her ex-boyfriend had given her and climbed into bed. She continued to read the book she had on her nightstand and she shortly fell asleep with the book still in her hands.

When Shantelle woke the next morning, she saw that all her shoes had moved to the side of the room furthest from the bed and that the small bell that had been hanging on the door was on her tallboy. She had not heard anything whilst she slept. She got out of bed and headed towards the toilet to relieve herself, but as she was walking past the mirror, she saw that it no longer showed a reflection of the room with her image missing, it now showed a tumultuous, swirling, vortex of light.

The mirror no longer reflected the room, nor was it just a mirror, it was still the same outward shape, but what was happening in the mirror, it did not look like the glass could contain it. A whirlpool of colors, spinning, contracting, expanding, dull then vibrant, dark then light, a maelstrom of colors preparing to tear the mirror and anything around it apart.

Shantelle wailed and her bladder opened where she stood. She collapsed into a puddle with wet underwear, legs and feet, though she did not notice it. She covered her face in her hands and wept long and hard.

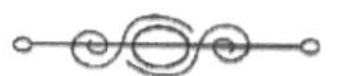

"So, my pretty, little girl," said Shantelle's uncle Col, in a very jovial manner, as he wrapped his arms around her and held her a little too close for her comfort, "What do you want for your 13th birthday, hey?"

Shantelle managed a grunt before her uncle Col squeezed her a bit tighter and moved his hands to get a better hold and said, "You'll be a teenager tomorrow, all grown up." Col called to his brother in-law, "Hey Bri, Brian," even louder, "Shanny brought any guys home yet?"

All Shantelle could do was grunt as she heard her mother Raylene yell from the kitchen, "Give it a fucking rest Col, she's only 13. She just had her first period last month."

"Mum!" said an angry Shantelle, "Why do you have to tell everyone?"

"I didn't tell everyone," said Raylene, "Just your Dad and uncle Col, both your grans and gramps and Sofia"

"Oh," said uncle Col lecherously, "you're a woman now. Well, the guys will be sniffing around pretty soon."

"Fucking leave it out Col," said an exasperated Raylene, "and I think you've been hugging her long enough."

Col released his niece just as a knock came to the flyscreen, "Yoo hoo, anyone home?" The flyscreen opened and in walked Sofia.

"Sofia!" said Raylene, "how good to see you. How have you been?"

Sofia smiled and said, "Good, good," as she walked around the room kissing first Raylene then Col, then her brother Brian and then Shantelle before turning and walking out the back flyscreen and kissing Bundy, the dog.

Shantelle had often heard her parents refer to her aunt Sofia as 'Crazy Sofia'. Sofia was just different from the rest of the Mason family and a lot different from her mum's family, the Brown's. Sofia was into Buddhism, Taoism and Wicca and other philosophies and teachings that no one in her family really understood. Sometimes she would show up at a family member's house and start doing some kind of ritual to bless the house or, cast out evil spirits. Lighting candles, burning incense, and chanting strange words. She didn't like to be called aunt or aunty and she said that when she had a child then that child could also call her Sofia because, everyone is and should be equal. We are all free souls, not tied to anyone or anything. This is why they thought she was crazy. Brock, Shantelle's 10 year old brother, was the last to come into the room. Brock had been in his bedroom on his X-Box. He was still wearing his headphones.

Now that everyone was assembled, Raylene got everyone to sit at the table for a birthday dinner and cake after. Raylene had made Shantelle's favorite food, lasagna with chips and salad. After the main meal, the gifts were given out. From her parents and her brother she received two CD's, two tops and a $20 voucher for Target. From uncle Col she got a card with $50 inside. From Sofia she got a little dragon figurine and a special card that Sofia said not to open until she was alone. After the presents, it was white chocolate cake with 13 candles.

At 8:30, Brock excused himself from the table and went back to his X-Box. The adults sat around and spoke about boring adult things and as Shantelle was getting bored, she excused herself, thanked and kissed everyone, narrowly avoided a grope from uncle Col, and headed to her room with her gifts.

Sofia called out to her. "Shantelle," she sauntered over and whispered, "I have given you a special wish inside your card, use it wisely and enjoy."

"Oi Sofia," called Brian, "I hope you're not filling Shanny's head with your hippy, witchcraft bullshit."

"Fuck off Brian," said Sofia. She turned to Shantelle and said, "Have a great birthday and I love you lots, you're my favorite niece."

Shantelle smiled and said, "That's because I'm your *only* niece."

Sofia smiled, kissed her cheek, turned away and started saying something to Raylene which Shantelle didn't catch as she made her way to her room.

Shantelle could hear Brock playing online from his bedroom as she walked by. She was thankful that the bathroom separated their rooms. She went into her room closed, the door, and wedged a bedside table against it.

Shantelle, like most 13 year olds, hated her parents and wanted to be away from them or them to be away from her. She hated her Mum and Dad for giving her such a stupid name, she wanted an ordinary name like... Jane or Emily, and she hated her little brother because he existed. She liked, loved her crazy aunt Sofia, and sometimes wished she could live with her.

She tried on the tops, put the $50 in her secret hidey-hole, in the pink frilly knickers right at the back, put on one of the best of CD's and placed the little dragon on her bookcase. She sat on her bed and opened the card from Sofia, in it was a note that said;

> *This is your real birthday gift.*
> *Repeat it 3 times and your wish*
> *should come true.*
> *With love and best wishes, Sofia.*
>
> *Gaia, Lilith, Ashtaroth and Baal,*
> *concede hoc unum donum dilexit*
> *exsultatiónis*

Shantelle smiled and thought, Sofia really is crazy, but she knew she had to try it. Since her 7th birthday, she had looked in the mirror and wondered what it was like on the other side. She had read 'Alice through the looking glass' and wanted that sort of adventure. She wished she could see around the corners of the full length mirror and see more of the reflected world.

Her Dad had 'found' the full length mirror at a new house being built a couple of streets away and had given it to Shantelle for her 7th birthday.

Shantelle sat in front of the mirror and read the words Sofia had written. First time nothing, second time nothing, third time, she felt nervous, but nothing happened. She placed her hand against the mirror but, it was just a mirror, she couldn't reach through, and she still couldn't see around the corners. She screwed up the note and threw it in the waste bin, grabbed a magazine and lay on her bed to read.

Shantelle was woken by a tapping noise, like a coin tapping against a window. She sat bolt upright, scared, looking everywhere for the sound of the tapping. She realized she had fallen asleep still dressed and her mum or dad had covered her with a blanket and turned off the music and the light. She turned on her bedside lamp and had another look around the room, at an oblique angle, she could see herself, looking out of the full length mirror.

She pulled the blanket up around her chin and almost screamed. She looked again and the face had gone from the mirror. She thought she must be having a bad dream and then she saw the little dragon Sofia had given her, rise up from the bookcase and sail over her bed, then over her head, then land gently on the floor near the mirror. Shantelle was scared but, she got out of bed and slowly walked to the mirror. Her reflection was there as it should be but, something didn't seem right, then her reflection spoke.

"Hello," her reflection said.

Shantelle took a panicked step back and gave a little scream. "What's happening?"

Her reflection smiled and said, "We made a wish and it looks like part of it came true. I am alive and so are you. I wonder if we can switch places."

Her reflection placed her hand against the mirror as Shantelle watched in fear as first a finger then the whole hand came through the mirror. "It's feels like jam or jelly or something. Come and try."

Shantelle walked to the mirror, put her hand against it and pushed. What her reflection said was true, it was like jam or jelly. Her reflection said, "Stand back, I'm going to try coming through."

Shantelle stood back as her reflection pushed and struggled to come through the mirror. She made it all the way through with a "Tada!" when she was pulled back to her side of the mirror faster than she came through. The sudden pull back to her side of the mirror left her in a heap on the floor. She turned to Shantelle and smiled.

"That was interesting," she said. "Maybe only one of us can be on each side of the mirror. Do you want to try switching sides?"

"I don't know," said Shantelle. "Does it hurt?"

"No it doesn't hurt, it just feels weird," her reflection said. "Come on, let's try and switch."

The reflection and Shantelle placed their hands on the mirror and then they slowly turned to their left. Shantelle could feel herself entering the mirror. Unlike the mirror itself, the liquid she seemed to be passing through felt warm and thick. They turned until they were both on the other side of the mirror, then they took their hands off the mirror, and nothing happened. They both stayed on the opposite side.

Shantelle's reflection started laughing which caused Shantelle to smile and start to laugh. "We did it!" said her reflection "We're in the mirror! Now we can find out what it's like in the mirror world, see if it's any different. Why don't I stay in here and you in there and we'll swap places again at noon tomorrow."

"Are you sure that's okay? What if something goes wrong?" said a worried Shantelle.

"What could go wrong? It's Sunday so there's no school and we don't have to see anyone but the family," said her reflection.

"Okay..." said Shantelle, "but don't forget, noon tomorrow."

"How could I forget, we're the same person," said her reflection.

Shantelle and her reflection had a look around each other's room, looking at all the differences. To both of them everything just seemed backward. The bed was on the wrong side, the door, the posters on the wall and all the books and CD's were written backward. Even the money was backward. Eventually around 5am they both climbed into the other's bed and slept. They both noticed that they could still see a reflection in any other mirror in their room, they were two separate people.

Their mothers woke them up at 9 with a big kiss and a "happy birthday my little angel, come on, get up." They both rose from their beds, looked at themselves in the mirror, smiled and waved and wished each other good luck.

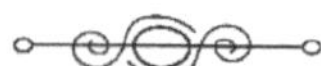

Shantelle walked around the house, everything was the same but opposite. Her parents were sitting in their chairs at the table but, the opposite way round. It was a bit confusing at first but Shantelle slowly got used to it. The hardest part of her breakfast was learning to use a knife and fork again, learning that the fridge opened the opposite way, same with the cupboards. Even everything on the TV was backward and the newspaper her reflection dad was reading was all written backward.

"Are you alright babe?" her mum asked, "You look a bit seedy. Did you have too much cake last night?"

"No mum," Shantelle replied "I didn't get much sleep last night because," then she yelled, "I'm a teenager now, woohoo!"

"Well, don't get too excited," said her dad. "No boyfriends till you're sixteen."

With a shrug, Shantelle finished her breakfast and went exploring. Everything she saw was opposite, the garden, the cars in the driveway and the cars themselves. The steering wheels were on the opposite side. She was amazed at how everything was the same only opposite, she wanted to keep exploring but, it was almost noon and she had to get back to the mirror and swap with her reflection.

Shantelle and her reflection met again at the mirror and swapped back to their own sides. Each one was gushing and telling the other about all the differences they had seen. They made a plan to do it again next weekend, this time for the whole weekend. During the week they would smile and talk to each other about all the things they wanted to do and see. When the weekend came around, they swapped sides again and they were both awestruck by the differences and sameness all around them. They still found it difficult to read signs but it was getting easier.

The reflection one day suggested that they swap sides on a school day. Shantelle was hesitant, but said yes. School was very hard. Shantelle was very slow at writing backward, the letters and numbers in reverse and reading the notes the teacher put on the board. It was fun and a bit stressful for Shantelle until she wrote a sentence her usual way. Her friends gathered round and watched as she did, what was to them, reverse writing very quickly. This was the best part of the day and later that evening, Shantelle and her reflection swapped back.

To try to ease the problem of reverse writing, Shantelle and her reflection sat facing each other and wrote out first the alphabet then numbers and then they tried full sentences. It was harder than they thought and they both got tired very quickly. They decided to only swap on weekends until they could reverse write well enough.

They swapped places almost every weekend for a few years and every once in a while a school day but, never longer than two days. Near her 16th birthday, her reflection suggested they swap for a week. A week of school and the weekend, swap Sunday night and return Sunday night. The reflection said they could still talk to each other through the mirror so if either of them got scared or wanted to return then there was no problem. Shantelle agreed.

Everything went fine for this weeklong swap until the reflection was asked out by Kieren Smedley, a year 11 boy. The reflection was excited but Shantelle didn't like Kieren very much and wanted her reflection to say no, but her reflection had already said yes, and they were going out

Friday night. Shantelle was scared; she didn't want to go out with Kieren and didn't want to have to break up with him when she returned to her own side. Her reflection told her not to worry, that she would let him down easy before the date was finished.

Her reflection did tell Kieren she wasn't interested but he asked Shantelle out the next week after they had swapped back. She said no but, unbeknown to her, her reflection was asking Kieren out on her side of the mirror. When they swapped places again, Shantelle didn't know why Kieren on the other side of the mirror was talking to her and wanting to catch up on the weekend. When she went back to her own side, the same thing was happening with her Kieren. Shantelle told her reflection to stop it, as it was making her look crazy. First wanting to go out and then saying no. Her reflection agreed to stop teasing Kieren.

Through high school, if either Shantelle or her reflection wanted to date someone, they had to check with the other. They would tell the boys that they could only see them at certain times because their parents were strict and they would swap places if it was a special date. When they went to university, they both had the same boyfriend for 18 months. He once in a while commented on their left or right handedness depending on who he was with. Shantelle and her reflection also commented on which was better for them; their real world or their reflective world.

After graduation, they both got jobs as graphic designers. With them both able to draw and write in reverse with ease, their employers thought it might be an asset to the company. They moved out of home and rented a two bedroom unit and took the mirror with them. Both Shantelle and her reflection loved their new job but, they both fancied different men in the company. Shantelle liked James, a balding man in his early 30's with the loveliest smile she had ever seen. Her reflection liked Tony, a 24 year old gym junkie with the classic Holden Monaro. Each guy had asked Shantelle and her reflection out and Shantelle and her reflection had a huge argument about who they would go out with.

Shantelle's reflection was yelling, "I want to go out with Tony and there is nothing you can do to stop me." She stormed out of the opposite room, slamming the door so hard that the little dragon fell off the tall boy.

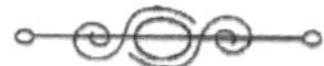

Shantelle stared at the mirror, a swirling vortex of light and color. She knew she could never go home. She felt helpless, and she knew her reflection must have done something to the mirror. Her real family would never know she was gone. She missed them very much, even though her family here were almost exactly the same. Shantelle sat in her room and watched the mirror to see if there would be any change. The colors kept swirling and pulsing then with a bright flash, the mirror went black. As she watched, the mirror slowly became a mirror again. She tried to talk to her reflection but, it was only a reflection.

Shantelle now had to get used to an Australia where, cars drove on the left hand side of the road and steering wheels were on the right. She had to keep writing from left to right and writing backward from how she was taught. She sometimes made mistakes writing an 'ɘ' or an 'ƨ' and some numbers backward.

She dated James a few times but thought he was an arrogant ass and now she lives alone with her cat Oscar in her 2-bedroom unit.

One Sunday, she went to her parents for Sunday roast. Roast pork with crackle, roast veggies and grandma's Yorkshire pudding. Sofia was there and she took Shantelle aside and whispered in her ear, "I know a little secret about you, but it will be all right now."

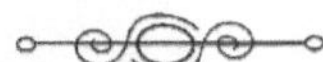

Concept idea given to authors to write story = a girl walks through a mirror into a world that is opposite. Not good and bad opposite, just left handed instead of right.

Conner Keegan is a 50 year old author whose stories have never been published. His stories never usually go further than my head or PC. His main motivation for writing is to stop the voices in his head. He most often sees the world he writes as an observer, but sometimes, especially with poetry, it is his own wants, desires and feelings that he channels.

When he thinks of a story, he structures it in my mind, but when he gets to writing it, the floodgates open and it could go anywhere. That is why he rarely shows his work to others.

He love to write and he believes that everyone has one great story to tell.

The Oceans

BY KRIS SOLBERG

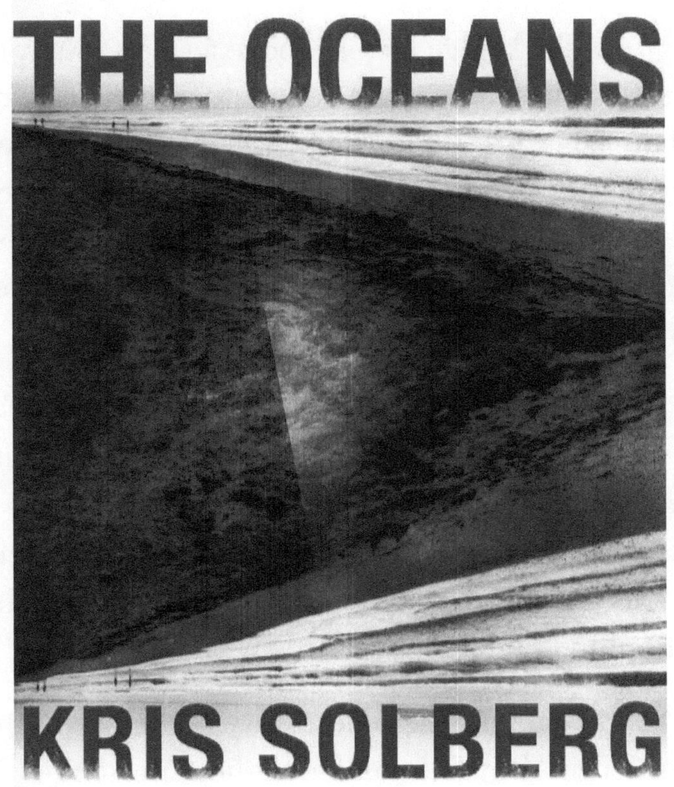

My feet tremble as I step onto the ledge, my toes cringe as they wrap themselves nervously around the railing. I quake as the wind throws itself around me, trying to force me off the ledge and back onto the condescending security of the asphalt below, yet I know this is my only chance for escape. It's my choice, my only choice.

The bridge towers above a steep valley, the grassy hills fall over the edge into a rocky canyon. The lights are swallowed by the darkness below. I can't see anything further down then the bridge. My feet quiver as another gush of wind thunders over me, but my hands clench with determination onto the ropes leading up to the roof of the bridge.

Enough staling, enough delaying, enough... of everything. I've come to terms with my end, with my death. I need to stop doubting myself, stop listening to the voices in my head. The ones telling me this is a rash decision, the ones telling me I shouldn't end it all because...because of her.

Yeah, it's the oldest story in the book. Boy meets girl, boy falls head over heels for girl, girl leaves boy for a handsome business man from Connecticut. I've seen this story unfold a million times in newspapers, books, magazines, movies, song lyrics, TV shows, video games, comics, cave paintings... It was never going to end in my favour, yet I believed her when she said we would last forever. I believed her, like the fool that I am, when she said she wouldn't leave me.

You see, this isn't the first time my skin has felt the cold, harsh affection of the 22nd street bridge. Two months ago, I stood here in the cold rain, clenching my fingers to the railing with a determined gaze aimed at the darkness waiting below. I was going to end it all.

Don't I sound melodramatic... any kind of struggle and I'll run to the closest bridge crying to the deafening blackness around me that 'I'll do it' and that 'I'm serious this time'. But I never had been, and to be perfectly honest, I wasn't that time either. I wasn't going to throw myself into oblivion over heartache, no matter how much I wanted to. But she didn't know that.

"You know what they say about people who commit suicide by jumping?" Her voice cut through the darkness with a bright, shiny knife. It bled with sincerity, affection and hope. She might not have said much at that point but from the very first syllable, I knew I was lost to her power, like a fly caught in a web.

"Does it matter?" My tone is harsh, snapping against the kindness of strangers. You might question my assessment, but remember I was never going to kill myself, so for someone to take the time to stop and try to talk me out of it, even in their own straightforward manner, meant something to me.

"It sure does." She stepped out of the darkness and into the light pouring down from the bridge, thundering down with the same force as the increasing rain. Her hair was soaking; her clothes bathing in the natural shower of Mother Nature, her face gleamed from the light hitting her face. "You see, they say that jumpers are the only people who commit suicide to experience all stages of grief before they die."

She walked closer to the railing, holding her hands outstretched as she placed her fingers upon the metal cable. Her body was about 20 feet away from me, yet I swear I smelt her lustrous scent. It was a mixture of wet dog and strawberries, a truly nauseating scent but in that moment it was the most magical thing ever to penetrate my nasal cavity.

"See, right now for instance, you are at the second stage; Anger. You're angry at someone, at everyone. You've already been through denial, promising yourself it will all get better eventually." Her words bore through me like a jack-hammer on cheese. I'm a piece of clay, waiting to be shaped at her command. "Soon, you'll begin bargaining with yourself, promising yourself that your pain will end if you just take one last step, but as you take that final step, you'll immediately get depressed. You will curse yourself for being rash, all of a sudden remembering all the things you love in life; family, friends, maybe even simpler things like a pizza overflowing with cheese. As you start remembering all of these things you will bury yourself deep within your own consciousness, trying to escape what is about to happen." She took a step towards me. It was a minimal movement and I hardly even noticed it. "Then... just before your face becomes a hollowed out, gushing fountain at the bottom of the canyon, you'll accept the hand you've dealt to yourself. You'll smile, briefly, making your last thought a happy one. Then you'll die."

I stared down at her from the ledge; she gazed up at me with warm, affectionate ocean blue eyes. I drowned in those eyes right then and there; I am still waiting to resurface.

"I just thought you wanted to know all the facts before you... you know, go for a dive into the empty pool." She smiled briefly before turning around. "Don't let me interrupt any longer".

"You haven't asked me why I'm killing myself..." She stopped on the edge of the light, her figure barely peering out of the darkness.

"Your reasons are your own." She turned a fraction of a circle, her cheek gleaming in the light once more. "If you want to kill yourself, well, who am I to stop you?"

She turned around and vanished into the darkness. I stood there on the edge, once again by myself, yet now my mind was working in overdrive. I felt a sea of emotion flood over me. I felt anger, sadness, despair, hope, curiosity, affection... love.

It was moronic, wasn't it? That in a span of less than five minutes I had fallen in love with a girl I didn't even know the name of. I remained on the ledge for what seemed like an eternity, every second feeling like a lifetime as I felt her warmth drift away from me. I couldn't take it any longer. I hurled myself from the ledge, landing coldly and harshly upon the concrete pavement.

You thought I killed myself, didn't you? Aren't you a depressing individual? You must be a hoot at scrabble, always finding words like 'morose' and 'carcass'. Anyway, enough about your failures as a human being, it's my love we're talking about here.

I chased after her into the darkness, yet as the light disappeared behind me I realised the foolishness of my pursuit. I didn't know anything about her. Not her name, where she lived, where she worked, nothing! I couldn't run around the city claiming to be looking for a girl with ocean blue eyes, with a smell combining wet dog and strawberries. How was I going to find her? How was I-

"Took you long enough" Her voice. It stopped the rain. For a second, her sound was the only thing showering over me.

"Who are you?" My voice is pleading, begging, yearning to learn the mysteries of her universe.

"Your worst nightmare." I saw her smile radiating out of the darkness, filling my world with light. "I'm just kidding; I've always wanted to say that."

"What's your name?" I took a step towards her voice, begging my eyes to hurry up and get accustomed to the black night.

"You'll never know, you'll never be able to guess." As she came into my field of vision, I saw her smile radiate even stronger than before. "Ah, come on, nothing? Rumplestiltskin...? ...you must've had a terrible childhood."

"Why did you save me?" I stood before her, feeling her breath on my skin.

"I didn't. You saved yourself."

I smiled "What's that from?"

"From me to you." I stared into her eyes, the ocean peering out of the darkness. "My name is-"

"No, no names. Not yet." Her face looked stern, with the hint of a smile breaking her pose.

"Why not?"

"Where's the fun in knowing everything?" She ran into the darkness, disappearing from my field of vision. "Come on, let's go."

"Go where?"

"To a place that matters."

I chased after her, with little aim and no sense of purpose. I chased her for what felt like hours, never stopping for rest, yet my body begging for a break. Finally, she stopped in front of a small swing in a park. She stared at the swing, before looking at my gasping, barely standing carcass.

"Someone needs to get into shape!" she chuckled as she got onto the swing. I watched as she began to swing back and forth, clinching her hands warmly to the metal chain holding up the little seat. She began to pick up momentum, laughing loudly as her body got closer and closer to the sky. Suddenly, her body leapt from the swing, soaring through the sky for a few moments before landing confidently in the sand dune below. "I've always loved the sensation of flying; the fear of falling followed by the joy of soaring. For those fleeting seconds, I am free."

She stared at me, my body finally able to stand upright, no longer looking like a retiree out and about without their walker. "Your turn" she declared as she began pulling me towards the swing.

"What? No, no, I ca-can't." My voice stammered nervously.

"Why not? You afraid of heights?" Her voice was condescending, sarcastic and cheerful all at once. It was a magnificent mixture of tone and emotion that still to this day remains unmatched. "Didn't seem that way earlier, you know, when you were about to hurl yourself into the abyss."

"Fine, you want me to fly, I'll fly." I walked towards the swing, feeling the chains dig into my thighs as I sat onto the little seat. My legs kicked against the sand as I started to gain momentum, rapidly increasing my pace.

Increasing...increasing...increasing...increasing...increasing...until...nothing.

I was falling, I had become a rag-doll waiting for the harsh embrace of the world below to tear me limb from limb. My heart had stopped, my blood piling against my veins, my lungs milking the last usage of the air still inside. Then... my eyes opened, my ears widened, my nostrils grew. I became one with the faltering wind. I became a bee, soaring through the skies above, harmoniously oblivious to the fact that I shouldn't be able to fly.

As my toes dug into the sand below me, I remained dormant for what felt like a year before bursting out of my cocoon, finally fluttering my wings. I gazed into her eyes, her beautiful, crystalline eyes. I belonged there, I felt at home in their warmth, in their affection, in their willingness to accept anything and everyone.

I leapt once more, only this time my lips dug into hers. They became one in the flickering light of a deserted park, the squeaky sounds of the swing still in motion, the only thing breaking the silence.

She pushed me away, ending my bliss.

"I----I-I-I can't." For the first time, I heard doubt in her voice. Insecurity resonating, echoing far beyond the passionate denial of my approach.

"Why not..?" My tone remained pleading, yearning for more.

"I...I just can't."

"Is there someone else?" My words were simple but my tone was complicated. It snarled more than it questioned. I didn't even know her name, yet I was treating her like some adulterous whore refusing to leave her husband for me.

"No... but you're not for me. You don't belong to me. You belong to someone else." What the hell was she talking about? My mind didn't get any time to catch up as she ran into the darkness.

"Wait... don't leave me! You CAN'T leave me!!" I hurled into the blackness.

"I didn't leave you, I was never here" She cried as she disappeared into the crushing darkness. The rain started again. Well, I suppose it had always been there but she had kept me safe, kept me dry.

I began drifting through the dark for minutes, hours, days, weeks, months. I was one with the blackness for what felt like a lifetime; however looking back it was more like two minutes.

That is how I ended up back at the bridge. Through my lost wandering, I returned to the place I met her. I don't know why. Maybe deep down I thought that if I returned to the bridge, the ledge, the edge, that she would save me again.

So maybe it wasn't two months ago... maybe she didn't leave me for a business man from Connecticut, but it's interesting the lies we tell others about ourselves to make us feel better.

Well, that about catches you up. I'm back on the ledge, waiting for her to save me again. I have been here for what feels like weeks but in reality has been seconds. I spent a lifetime with her, but in actual passage of time it was more like twenty minutes.

My feet remain on the edge, waiting for a command from the governing body of my little organisation. The wind is crying around me, the rain joining in the emotional turmoil that is the nightly strokes of this scene.

I am asking myself the big questions as I wait for her to save me. What did she mean that I didn't belong to her? Was she merely the messenger, telling me I had a future that I am about to throw away because she didn't fill in all the blanks? Was she a premonition of what I could have if I drag my mind out of the darkness? So many questions, yet so few answers.

In an attempt to convey a sense of danger to any eyes staring at me from the blackness, I dangle a foot above the ledge. My other foot slips on the wet railing and I go sailing over the railing. This time you're right. This time, I am falling to my death. I wait for her cry but nothing escapes the dark cloak of night.

I curse myself for challenging death. I would have had so much to live for if I didn't decide to push my luck. The wind around me is picking up, slowly gaining momentum as the stuttering rain gains confidence and grows into a fully fleshed out storm. I yearn for the wind to save me, to push me back onto the ledge, but nothing changes. I am still plunging to my death, feeling my skin grow cold as the ground below me is getting more visible.

As the ground grows bigger, I forget about my regrets, my lost chances. I forget about all the times I could have acted differently, should have done something in a different way. I remember her, still a captive of her eyes, still drowning in those oceans. As my remaining moments count down, I only remember her. I smile, briefly as I remember the huge amount of influence she had on my life in such a short timespan... then I die.

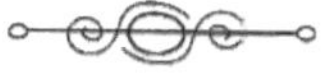

Concept idea given to authors to write story = A man stands at the edge of a bridge, looking down at the vicious waves below. He crunches a photo in his hand, a photo marking his past, marking the reason that brought him to this dark place. With the rain thundering down around him, he waits for something he fears will never come.

Kris Soldberg is an Author with a passion for exploring the dark corners of his mind through writing.

Epilogue

BY **B**EN **R**OSE NTH AL

Saturday (I think).
And here I am. I don't know how many days — or months — I've been out here. That's the problem travelling through countless alternate realities; too many calendars.
But I'm almost home.
I'm still not sure if I'm pleased with that.
...

I should proof-read this. Go back over the stories. Make sure I haven't left anything out; given credit to those brave enough to help us on our way. Correct the obvious speeling errors.

Nah.

But what to do now? Do I sell my story? Would anyone believe it if I did? Could the tale of a simple guy standing on top of a cliff getting shoved (literally) into an adventure through the multiverse be seen as anything but fiction?

Closing my journal I think of all that has happened. Of the adventures. Of Phil and his collection of suits. And of Jasmine. Always Jasmine. Of all that we both found and lost. Of all that she has lost. I am not sure if it is this new life of excitement I am sad to be leaving, or that she will be leaving mine.

Rising from my chair I take in the surroundings of my makeshift room. Mementos scattered along the shelving. I say mementos, but they are more than that. They are trophies. Rewards for what I have done. The black scarf of Cratochek. The tribal headdress of the proud people of Hinderndan. That level ten Sudoku puzzle I finally beat. All of them hold memories for me. All of them now a part of me.

At that moment my door slides open. A head of brown re-growth devouring a once pink Mohawk stands before me. "David", she speaks excitedly. "We've found her!"

"Wha...? No! Does that mean...?"

"Yup," Jasmine replies. Her bright smile already lifting the heavy feeling from my chest. "You're stuck with me for a bit longer."

I walk towards her as Jasmine turns from my cramped quarters.

"Now, let's get her back," she yells with joy as she runs down the small corridor to the control room.

I take my seat next to Jasmine. The vastness of space spreads out before me. We thought we had lost her, but she is within our sights again. We are back on the trail of Small Dragon.

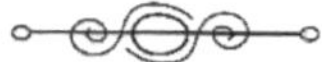

Ben Rosenthal was born from a young age. His hobbies include reading, writing and referring to himself in the third person.

You can see more of his words at ManInSuitComics.com, benjum.com or hassle him over on twitter: @BenRosenthal.